Skira Guides

Skira Guides

The Brera Gallery

Introduction by Sandrina Bandera
Entries by Paola Strada

Front Cover
Umberto Boccioni, *Riot at the Gallery*,
1910; Francesco Hayez, *The Kiss*, 1859;
Raphael (Raffaello Sanzio), *Marriage
of the Virgin*, 1504 (details)

Facing title page
Raphael (Raffaello Sanzio), *Marriage
of the Virgin*, 1504 (detail)

Editor
Eileen Romano

Design
Marcello Francone

Editorial Coordination
Carla Casu

Editing
Maria Conconi

Layout
Anna Cattaneo

Translations
Richard Burns for Language Consulting
Congressi, Milan

Photographies
works: Archivio fotografico
della Soprintendenza B.S.A.E. di Milano /
by permission of the Ministero
per i Beni e le Attività Culturali
halls: Paolo Manusardi, Milano
© Carlo Carrà, Filippo de Pisis,
Arturo Martini, Giorgio Morandi,
Alberto Savinio, Mario Sironi
by SIAE 2010
© Succession Picasso
by SIAE 2010
All rights reserved

First published in Italy in 2010 by
Skira Editore S.p.A.
Palazzo Casati Stampa
via Torino 61
20123 Milano
Italy

www.skira.net

© 2010 Ministero per i Beni
e le Attività Culturali / Soprintendenza
B.S.A.E.
© 2010 Skira editore, Milano
All rights reserved
© 2010 by Skira editore

ISBN 978-88-572-0454-3

www.skira.net

Printed and bound in Italy. First edition

Contents

Introduction
*Sandrina Bandera**

*Director
of the Pinacoteca
di Brera

In its initial conception, the Pinacoteca di Brera was a collection of works providing support for the training of young artists at the Academy of Fine Arts. Its actual birth, however, was an initiative of the Napoleonic government in Italy to create a Royal Gallery based on the model of emerging national museums such as the Louvre. It was officially inaugurated on the 15th of August 1809, Napoleon's birthday. Napoleon, at the time king of Italy and Emperor of France, had contributed to the creation in Milan of an important nucleus of masterpieces from central and northern Italy, especially Venetia and Lombardy, with the aim of creating a museum that would glorify his power and inspired by the modern ideals of the French Revolution. Since the museum was opened, a number of its rooms have housed and exhibited the Academy's collections of plaster casts, paintings and engravings. The rest was dedicated to a "political" collection of paintings, i.e., a collection amassed by the State, coming from the churches suppressed and looted as Napoleon's army made its way through the territory.

The Brera Fine Arts Academy was founded in 1776, by volition of Maria Theresa, in Palazzo Brera, next to the Humiliati church of Santa Maria di Brera. The palazzo had been home to a Jesuit college that was suppressed in 1772. The building, undergoing construction since the late 16th century, had just attained its current guise with the work of the Neoclassical architect Giuseppe Piermarini. At that time, as today, the Palazzo di Brera housed important cultural institutions: the Astronomy Observatory, the Library and the Medicinal Garden. In addition to these, beside the Academy, the Austrian empress also instituted the Lombard Academy of Science and Letters.

Thanks to the sensitivity and commitment of people of the calibre of Giuseppe Bossi, painter and Academy secretary, and Andrea Appiani,

The courtyard of honour with the bronze statue of *Napoleon as Mars the Pacifier* by Antonio Canova.

7

painter, commissioner of Fine Arts and curator, the new museum gained respect as an educational facility and as an institution that preserved and made available to the public an inestimable legacy of art. This heritage would grow significantly through exchanges, bequests and donations throughout the nineteenth century and beyond. The walls of the few rooms then available on the *piano nobile* were soon filled with paintings displayed in new uniform gilt frames in two orders to create a gallery effect, with care given to symmetries of formats and subjects. The collection was dominated by works of Venetian and Lombard artists from the 15th to the 18th century in small, medium and large formats (there are many altarpieces), immediately recognised as true masterpieces. After Italian unification contest submissions were added – and would continue to arrive as the decades passed –, canvases by contemporary painters, teachers and pupils from the Milanese Academy.

Since it opened, the museum has been situated in its current location in the grand first-floor halls still known as the "Saloni Napoleonici". These were created by building a floor in the nave of the Medieval church of Santa Maria di Brera, which had been suppressed in 1808. The Napoleonic Halls were chosen for the placement of the plaster statue of *Napoleon as Mars the Pacifier*, a work by the renowned sculptor Antonio Canova. Like the cast bronze work in the centre of the court of honour, this statue was strongly desired by Eugène de Beauharnais, Napoleon's adopted son and viceroy of the Kingdom of Italy, an enthusiastic art lover and collector. In 2009, the colossal statue was replaced in the court of honour after being restored, welcoming visitors while underscoring the bond between Napoleon and the museum.

In the years 1809-11, an impressive spate of confiscated works from Veneto, Emilia-Romagna and The Marches were added to the collections (over one thousand works in three years, all needing to be registered, attributed, selected and placed on display or in storage). Also starting in the early nineteenth century, a number of key Milanese Renaissance works began to arrive. These included frescoes by Gaudenzio Ferrari, Bernardino Luini and Bergognone, removed from the walls of churches and city residences using procedures pioneered by Lombard restoration workshops. The Brera Gallery is one of the world's best endowed museums for this type of figurative documentation.

The many works that the museum was unable to exhibit, due to space constraints, were from early on deposited with Milanese and Lombard churches to refit altars that had been stripped not so long before. Others, whose quality and importance were not fully appreciat-

Following pages:
Room XXXVII with
its 19th-century
paintings.

ed, were traded through antiquarians or directly with European museums to obtain works of artists otherwise absent from the galleries. The generous bequest of Pietro Oggioni in 1855 represents the first major acquisition of a private collection by the museum.

It was only in 1882, under the directorship of Giuseppe Bertini, that the two institutions (Gallery and Academy) would be officially separated. However, it was agreed that the museum would continue to exhibit in the same spaces the original nuclei of the respective collections. At the beginning of the 20th century, the Brera Gallery reopened with a new exhibition design developed by the director Corrado Ricci. The green wallpapered galleries arranged in a ring around the courtyard of honour exhibited many paintings that had not previously been displayed. Now for the first time the works were arranged by regional school and chronological order, adhering to scientific criteria developed in that period; this arrangement is the closest to that found in the museum today. Zenith lighting was obtained by bricking up most of the windows and installing new skylights.

During the same period, Milan also opened to the public the municipal collections in Castello Sforzesco, which drew in the Medieval and Renaissance sculptures of the Museo di Storia Patria, which had been kept for almost a century in the deconsecrated nave of Santa Maria di Brera. Moreover, the Academy and the Brera Gallery contributed with a loan of works to the inauguration of the first nucleus of works of the Galleria d'Arte Moderna (Civic Gallery of Modern Art).

During the First World War the Brera Gallery was closed and emptied of paintings. The museum reopened in 1925, revealing the elegant restoration work of the architect Piero Portaluppi, who renovated in Neo-Renaissance style the rooms housing masterpieces such as Raphael's *Marriage of the Virgin*, and embellished the other galleries with the use of fine materials: a variety of marbles for the plinth course and jambs of the passageways between the rooms and Corinthian capitals on the columns separating the Napoleonic Halls. He also rebuilt the chapel of San Giuseppe which was formerly in the church of Santa Maria della Pace, with frescoes by Bernardino Luini.

The Friends of Brera Association, constituted in 1927, supported the museum with significant donations: one among them all, *Supper at Emmaus* by Caravaggio – who was rediscovered by critics precisely in those years –, reached the museum thanks to a synergistic relationship between the superintendent Ettore Modigliani and the president of the Friends of Brera, Ettore Conti. In the 20th century, a number of collectors in the Association's orbit donated works from their pri-

9

vate collections to the Gallery, allowing it to continue growing. Brera was closed again when the Second World War broke out. The paintings were sequestered away in crates and after a few months they began a peregrination among various refuges chosen by the Superintendent and his appointed functionary according to developments in the conflict and the perceived level of threat to people and property. They were initially kept in villas on Lake Maggiore, then in fortresses in the Marches, and lastly in the Vatican in Rome, together with a multitude of masterpieces from other museums, private collections and many churches in occupied and divided Italy.

The reopening in 1950 was preceded by new restoration work in the galleries, which had suffered serious damage during the bombing raids of 1943. Ettore Modigliani was again one of the principal minds behind the effort, replaced later by Fernanda Wittgens. The architect was once again Piero Portaluppi. Some of the rooms underwent radical transformation, many of the ceilings were modified. Prized marbles were obtained from the Opificio delle Pietre Dure in Florence. The lighting was completely redesigned. For example, in the Napoleonic Halls, the cross-shaped roof windows were replaced with large "Neoclassical" domes. Franco Albini arranged Lombard and Venetian easel paintings on partition walls in a continuous gallery,

Room XIV with 16th-century Lombard and Venetian paintings. In the centre, the plaster statue of Napoleon by Antonio Canova.

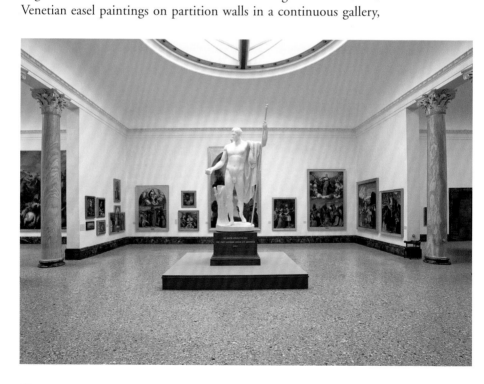

corresponding to the modern-day Room X, using a novel form of indirect lighting which can still be seen in the long white "sails" that screen the natural light.

In the 1970s, under the direction of Franco Russoli, the museum went through a period of crisis and rethinking, marked by a polemical closing of the doors, innovative and provocatory exhibitions, the first expansion projects into Palazzo Citterio (initiating talk of the future "Grande Brera"), the ill-fated loan of works from the Jucker collection (subsequently acquired by the City of Milan), and the extraordinary donation of a highly select group of 20th-century masterpieces from the Jesi collection.

Carlo Bertelli's stewardship in the 1980s brought about a significant turning point: the first museum bookshop and café in Italy were inaugurated and climate-controlled storage rooms where the works could be viewed were built. A substantial museum reorganisation project was undertaken and continued into the mid-1990s, with a number of operations directed by the architect Vittorio Gregotti. In the first years of the 21st century, the extraordinary Vitali collection was also exhibited, which included a variety of works: sculpture, painting, and mosaics expressing a variety of different cultures and different eras, reaffirming the exhibition tradition inaugurated with the Jesi collection to keep major bequests intact, making an exception to the traditional subdivision by school of painting.

For the bicentennial of the birth of the museum (2009) and during the following year, the exhibition design was reworked in a number of the rooms, proposing new juxtapositions of paintings and adding a number of works that had previously been in storage. For those familiar with the Gallery, this reinterpretation is particularly evident in the rooms dedicated to nineteenth-century paintings, Lombard painters of the 15th and 16th centuries and the polyptychs from the Marches. The new colour scheme in all the rooms along the ring and experimentation with direct lighting of works in most of the rooms – with substantial funding from the City of Milan –, is meant to enhance the visitor's sense of continuity moving through the museum and facilitate the perception and appreciation of its extraordinary works.

Notice
It being impossible to provide
an exhaustive description of all
the works in the museum, this guide
to the collections of the Gallery
proposes a selection of works chosen
to exemplify the art exhibited in each
room. In order to facilitate reference,
the guide is organised in accordance
with the numbering of the rooms.
The text has been prepared by
Paola Strada and the museum
educational department. The curator
would also like to thank Emanuela
Daffra, Roberto Giuranna, Isabella
Marelli and Cristina Quattrini.

Visit

Room I

The long corridor, added to the museum's itinerary in 1903, contains frescoes by two of the protagonists of Renaissance art in Milan during the Sforza duchy, Donato Bramante and Bernardino Luini. *Men at Arms*, a work painted by Bramante from Urbino *circa* 1486–87, entered the Brera collections in 1901–02. The fresco was and originally in a dwelling on Via Lanzone belonging in the late 15th century to the poet and ducal counsellor Gasparo Visconti. New for its time were the monumental conception of the figures and the illusionistic effects, which would find greater currency in early 16th-century Lombard painting. Originally full height figures viewed from a low angle, the characters with their well defined features tower within false niches. The presence of the *Poet* and the *Laureate* suggests an iconography associated with the owner's close circle of acquaintances, which included the Bramante himself.

In 1821–22 the Pinacoteca acquired the main group of Bernardino Luini's frescoes, which once decorated the walls of three rooms and the ground floor chapel of Villa Pelucca, the suburban abode of the nobleman Gerolamo Rabia since 1506, now engulfed by the city of Sesto San Giovanni. Stefano Barezzi was responsible for removing the frescoes and transferring them onto wooden panels, an incomplete operation that has irremediably compromised our ability to understand some of the portrayed subjects. Datable to the end of the first or beginning of the second decade of the 16th century, the frescoes by the Milanese painter celebrate nature as the setting for myths and the promised land of the Old Testament in keeping with his patron's interests. Three thematic nuclei are found at the Pinacoteca: mythological scenes; the cycle of the flight of the Jews from Egypt; and the courtly games.

Bernardino Luini
(1480/82–1532)
The Jews' Song of Triumph
Fresco transferred onto panel,
243 x 143 cm

The fresco was part of the decorations with the story of Exodus in the main hall on the ground floor of Villa Pelucca. In the foreground we see the Jews singing praises after their miraculous crossing of the Red Sea guided by Moses. The space dedicated to the landscape may reflect the patron's and the painter's interest in ancient and contemporary architectural treatises. The visible cracks are the result of the transferral of the fresco onto panel, a practice which was later abandoned.

Donato Bramante (Donato di Pascuccio
d'Antonio known as), (1444–1514)
Heraclitus and Democritus
Fresco transferred onto canvas, 102 x 127 cm

The famous fresco of the ancient
philosophers *Heraclitus and Democritus*
was once located above the door in a
different room from the one containing the
Men at Arms: one weeps and the other
laughs at human folly while in the middle a
globe reproduces a part of the earth's
surface as it was then known.

Donato Bramante
(Donato di
Pascuccio d'Antonio
known as),
(1444–1514)
*Man with
Broadsword*
Fresco transferred
onto canvas,
285 x 127 cm

The immense, virile
figure wearing a
ceremonial armour
under his long red
cape was originally
holding a
broadsword. It is
located in an
elaborate semi-
circular niche,
decorated with
pilaster strips and a
classical frame,
which appeared to
extend beyond the
walls of the
"chamber of
barons".

Room I A

The presbytery of the oratory of Santa Maria in Mocchirolo (near Lentate on the Seveso River in Brianza) was reconstructed in the museum in 1949 to display its frescoes – which had been removed from the walls and donated to the Pinacoteca using a procedure that has since come under criticism – in their rightful context. The frescoes in the family chapel of Count Lanfranco Porro document the orientation of the nobles in the Visconti court in the latter half of the fourteenth century toward Tuscan painting, and especially to the followers of Giotto. The painter of the Mocchirolo cycle may be Pecino da Nova, whom documents state painted in "Moncayrolum" in 1378. Like the frescoes in other Lombard oratories of the same time, the scenes are characterised by a narrative style richly evocative of manners and settings, with echoes of the painting of Giovanni da Milano and Giusto de' Menabuoi.

Master of Mocchirolo (active in Lombardy in the second half of the 14th century)
Count Porro and Family offering a Model of the Church to the Virgin Fresco transferred onto canvas, 323 x 217 cm

Lanfranco Porro's entire family is depicted in profile on the right-hand wall, kneeling in feudal and votive homage to the enthroned Madonna. The count offers the Virgin a model of the oratory. The delicate colours and the realistic faces of the characters stand out clearly.

The Mocchirolo Chapel.

Room II

The room is the first in a group of small galleries restored in 1986–87 by the architect Vittorio Gregotti. The current exhibition setup, which dates to 1995–96, features the few and highly select paintings owned by the museum from the early centuries of "modern" painting, before and after Giotto. They are gold-ground paintings, almost all of them by 14th-century painters mainly from Tuscany. They include the rare small panels by Giovanni Baronzio of Rimini (*Stories of Saint Columba*), Barnaba of Modena and the Giottoesque Bernardo Daddi (*Saint Lawrence*) which were once part of altar frontals and altarpieces. In addition to the triptych reliquary by Bartolomeo and Jacopino da Reggio and the important small altarpiece by Lorenzo Veneziano, in its original frame, of particular note are the 13th-century altar frontal with Saint Veranus, still characterised by the "Byzantine" style, and two 14th-century masterpieces, *Madonna with Child* by Ambrogio Lorenzetti of Siena, donated in 1947 by Guido Cagnola, and *Christ the Judge* from the Contini Bonacossi collection, acquired for the Pinacoteca in 1970 by the Friends of Brera. Before going to Tuscany, Cagnola, of Lombard origin, had occasion to familiarise himself with the novelty of Giotto's painting in the 1330s, when the Florentine painter was in Milan. In 2008, the small collection was enriched with the two panels of Saint Lawrence and John the Baptist that were once part of a now disassembled late 14th-century polyptych by the Tuscan painter Spinello Aretino.

Master of San Verano (active from circa 1270 to 1275) Saint Veranus between Two Angels and Six Scenes from his Life Tempera on panel, 152 x 97 cm

Datable to circa 1275, the work may have once been in the Pieve di San Verano in Peccioli, near Pisa. In the rare altar frontal, the saint is portrayed frontally against a gold background and is flanked by vivid scenes and miraculous episodes in his life, from his baptism at the upper left to his burial at lower right. The three-dimensional effects as well as the interplay of light and shadow are accomplished by creating adjacent or overlapping colour fields with no gradation.

Giovanni da Milano (documented between 1346 and 1369)
Christ the Judge worshipped by Angels, 1360–65
Tempera on panel, 152.3 x 68.5 cm

This was the central panel of a polyptych created by the Giottoesque painter probably for the Camaldolite convent of Santa Maria degli Angeli in Florence. Christ, with a very human, softly contoured face, is depicted according to the apocalyptic iconography as the king of Justice, in the act of giving his blessing while solemnly seated on a faldstool with leonine armrests, alluding to the temporal power of the popes.

Ambrogio Lorenzetti
(1285–1348)
Madonna and Child
Tempera on panel,
85 x 57 cm

In this youthful work, the artist from Siena concentrated on the sentimental relationship between the two figures. Although no longer in prime condition, this central polyptych panel is striking for the tenderness in the eyes of the Madonna, elegantly draped in brocade, as she gazes upon her son. The child wiggles his feet in the swaddling clothes, his hand and foot skilfully foreshortened.

Rooms III-IV

These two rooms contain a number of significant exemplars of the so-called International Gothic style, a figurative style that gained popularity toward the end of the 14th century and remained in vogue for most of the 15th, with similar characteristics among all the principal European courts and many smaller cities. From Paris to Prague and from Avignon to Milan, the painters faithfully reproduced their subjects, with a particular emphasis on surfaces, fabrics and precious ornaments, oftentimes transforming sacred subjects into images dominated by profane worldly luxury. The *Valle Romita Polyptych* is a true masterpiece, painted by Gentile da Fabriano, one of the preeminent artists in the fertile artistic climate of his times, in the early years of the 15th century. The *Crucifixion*, acquired in 1995 and displayed next to it, may have been part of the polyptych. In the *Madonna and Child* by Jacopo Bellini, one of Gentile's Venetian students, we note more clearly modern features, such as a more careful execution of volumes and spaces. The refined colours and soft lines of figures and fabrics that characterise the *Valle Romita Polyptych* are also seen in the works of Pere Serra from Catalonia (*Annunciation*), Stefano da Verona and those of painters active in the Sforza court in Lombardy, such as Bonifacio Bembo and the Zavattari brothers (*Assumption of the Virgin*).

Gentile da Fabriano (*circa* 1370–1427)
Valle Romita Polyptych, 1408–10
Tempera on panel. Central panel,
157 x 79 cm; lower side panels, 117 x 40 cm;
upper side panels 49 x 38 cm.

This work entered the collections in 1811
from the hermitage of Santa Maria
di Valdisasso, near Fabriano.
Recomposed in a Neo-gothic frame, the
polyptych was probably commissioned

by the local lord, Chiavello Chiavelli and
created in Venice. A subject and
iconography dear to the Franciscans, the
Coronation of the Virgin occupies the
centre above the choir of angels playing
music while kneeling on the celestial vault
and is complemented by full figure images
of saints and small narrative scenes.
The gold in the background, the clothing
and halos was applied using a variety
of refined techniques.

Details of the *Valle Romita Polyptych*.

Stefano da Verona (*circa* 1375 – *post* 1438)
Adoration of the Magi, 1435–36
Tempera on panel, 72 x 47 cm

Among the Italian protagonists of the
International Gothic style, in this work from
his mature years, Da Verona sets the
sacred subject in a fairy tale atmosphere,
emphasised by the splendour of the gifts
offered to the Child, the sumptuousness
of the Magi's clothing and the realistic
portrayals of the people and animals in
procession. The smaller scenes in the
background also teem with details.
The two flowers in the foreground evoke
the miniated herbals found in fourteenth-
century codices.

Bonifacio Bembo (*circa* 1420 – at least until 1477)
Saint Alexius and Saint Julian
(or *Saint James*), 1463–70
Tempera on panel, 85 x 28 cm each

Painted by Bembo when he was the official artist for the court of Galeazzo Sforza, these are the side panels of a disassembled polyptych. The two saints, wearing minutely reproduced fashionable clothes, seem barely to touch the ground. The meadow is filled with different species of plants and herbs painted with extreme precision.

Jacopo Bellini (*circa* 1400–1470/71)
Madonna and Child, 1448
Tempera on panel, 50 x 45 cm

The small panel, originally part of a polyptych in the Church of the Visitation in Casalfiumanese (Bologna), has been in the collection since 1912. It is signed and dated on the faux polylobate marble frame. The Venetian Jacopo Bellini, father of Gentile and Giovanni, absorbed the new Renaissance artistic lexicon by simplifying his volumes and introducing a modern rendition of space.

31

Room V

With the exception of the canvas by the Spaniard Pedro Berruguete, this room is dedicated to paintings on wood from north-eastern Italy, created between the second half of the 15th century and the first decades of the 16th. The artists who painted them strove to reconcile their inherited figurative tradition with the novelties of the Renaissance style, introduced in Padua by the sculptor Donatello and then spread through the Venetian Republic. These efforts may be discerned in the *Praglia Polyptych*, an early 15th-century Venetian work from the important bottega of Antonio Vivarini and his son-in-law Giovanni d'Alemagna: within the traditional structure we note the volumetric execution of the figures. Another example is *Saint Mark* by Master Giorgio, caught between features proper to Byzantine icons and the innovative style embodied in characters painted by his contemporary Andrea Mantegna.

Antonio Vivarini (*circa* 1418–1476/84) and Giovanni d'Alemagna (documented between 1437 and 1450) *Praglia Polyptych*, 1448–50 Tempera on panel, 114 x 165 cm

The polyptych comes from the main altar of a Benedictine abbey located near Padua. The abbot, Cipriano Rinaldini, is portrayed, in a reduced scale, kneeling before the volumetric figures of the Virgin and Child on the throne in the central panel. The full-figure saints stand on foreshortened circular bases in the frameless polyptych.

Pedro Berruguete (*circa* 1450 – *circa* 1504)
Dead Christ supported by two Angels, 1480
Oil on canvas, 71 x 62 cm

Placed in this room because it was
thought to come from the Venetian Church
of Charity, the canvas actually originated
in the convent of Sant'Agata Feltria near
Urbino. The painter – Spanish but with
a Flemish pictorial style – sojourned
in Urbino in 1472 in the court of Federico
da Montefeltro, for whom he painted
portraits of illustrious men for the small
studio in Palazzo Ducale. He also
contributed to the altarpiece by Piero
della Francesca.
In keeping with an iconography that
was common especially in Flanders,
two angels support Christ in the sepulchre,
offering him to our meditation.

33

Room VI

Together with room VII, this gallery occupies a corridor designed by Vittorio Gregotti, who chose to align Mantegna's *Dead Christ* with the axis of the previous rooms, keeping in mind the constraints dictated by the foreshortening of the figure. This gallery is dedicated to medium-format Renaissance Venetian paintings, datable to the period from the second half of the 15th century to the first decades of the following, and contains some of the greatest masterpieces of Italian art. The crowning masters are Andrea Mantegna of Padua and Giovanni Bellini of Venice: their works, spanning their entire artistic careers from youth to full maturity, are placed side by side on the same wall and at times engage in close dialogue, as we see between Mantegna's *Madonna of the Cherubim* and Bellini's *Greek Madonna*, both acquired by the Pinacoteca in 1808.

The large canvases by Vittore Carpaccio, with the *Presentation of the Virgin in the Temple*, the *Marriage of the Virgin* and the *Disputation of Saint Stephen*, narrative compositions crowded with people in imaginary urban settings, attest to the typically Venetian tradition of paintings created to decorate the seats of the *Scuole*, lay confraternities dedicated to providing services and charity work.

Beside them we see *Saint Jerome in the Desert* and the small altarpiece with *Saint Peter Enthroned*, both painted by Cima da Conegliano. Younger than Giovanni Bellini, whose works he studied, Cima created peaceful and majestic images immersed in landscapes of luminous beauty.

Andrea Mantegna (*circa* 1430–1506)
Polyptych of Saint Luke, 1453–54
Tempera on panel, 177 x 230 cm

A youthful work, the polyptych was done for the chapel of San Luca in the Benedictine church of Santa Giustina in Padua. While remaining within the traditional structure of the polyptych – a number of different panels with gold backgrounds – the painter adopted Renaissance-style solutions in his rendition of space. The austere saints in the first order stand on a single step painted in perspective, while the volumetric figures of the upper order are viewed from below as if they were looking out from a loggia. The materials of the lectern and throne are reproduced mimetically while the faces of the characters amount to true portraits.

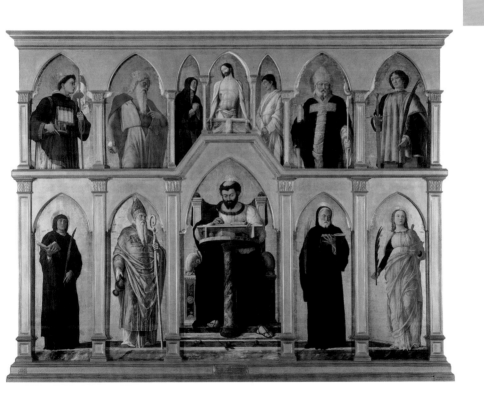

Andrea Mantegna (*circa* 1430–1506)
Dead Christ
Tempera on canvas, 68 x 81 cm

This very delicate *tempera magra* (pigment mixed with animal glues) work is probably the *Cristo in scurto* (*Foreshortened Christ*) that was still in the artist's studio in Mantua when he died in 1506. Christ's body, viewed from approximately the height of his pierced hands, is lying on the unction stone in preparation for burial, draped in his shroud. To the left John, elderly Mary and a pious woman, perhaps Mary Magdalene, are weeping. The colour scheme is reduced to the essential: greys, browns and ochre; the drawing is skilfully realistic. Christ's head is over-proportioned with respect to the foreshortened body in order to keep it clearly readable.

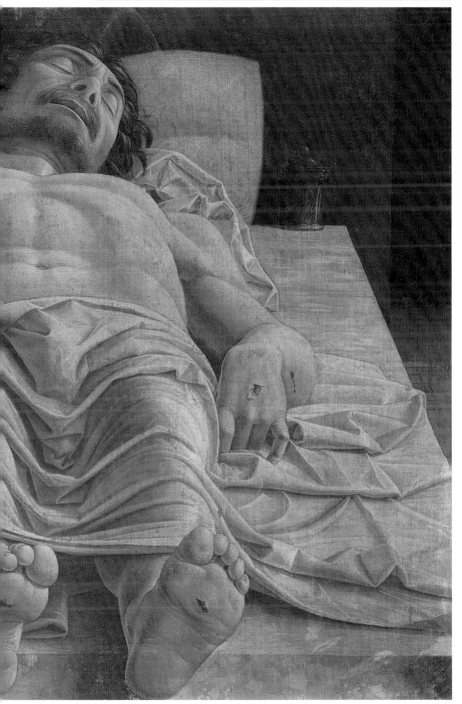

HAEC FERE QVM GEMITVS TVRGENT
BELLINI POTERAT FLERE IOANNIS OP

Giovanni Bellini
(*circa* 1430–1516)
Pietà
Tempera on panel,
86 x 107 cm

Donated to Brera in 1811 by the viceroy Eugène de Beauharnais, the famous panel shows the influence of the artist's brother-in-law Andrea Mantegna in the power of the starkly outlined figures. The lifeless body of Christ is supported by the Virgin and Saint John in the marble sepulchre against a landscape under a grey sky. In the 1460s, Bellini placed the accent on the emotional bonds between the protagonists, uniting Mother and Son into a single unit.

IOANNES
BELLINVS
MDX

Giovanni Bellini (*circa* 1430–1516)
Madonna and Child, 1510
Oil on panel transferred onto canvas,
85 x 115 cm

Immersed in the atmospheric light of the
soft Venetian countryside, the *Madonna
and Child* was painted when Bellini was
eighty years old. With the preparatory
sketch reduced to a few bold lines,
following the dictates of the early 16th-
century Venetian painting style, the
characters and elements are constructed
from thickly or thinly spread oil paint. The
apparent simplicity of the subject is called
into question by the cheetah on the marble
cippus, which would allude to sin, and by
the twigs smeared in birdlime and the bird
tethered as bait on the right, which would
refer to the Passion of Christ.

The select group of 16th-century portraits from the modern-day regions of Veneto and Friuli-Venezia Giulia, document the progression of the local genre toward more subtle psychological renderings, while still underscoring the character's social position through a faithful reproduction of features, clothing and accessories. A clear example of this dual function is the *Portrait of an Elderly Gentleman with Gloves*, perhaps Liberale da Pimentel, painted by Lorenzo Lotto in the 1540s. His melancholic face, in full light, softly marked by age, signifies his high rank, as do his clothing, ring, gold watch chain, embroidered handkerchief and the gloves he is holding. The Brera collections contain four of this artist's most important portraits. Three of them were acquired in 1859 through Francesco Hayez with funds provided by King Vittorio Emanuele II. The three-quarter view of the figure, typical of Venetian portraits, is seen in various works, including the podestà *Bergamo Antonio Navagero* by Giovanni Battista Moroni, resolved in a very spontaneous fashion. The only self-portrait here is that of Palma the Younger, who depicted himself bold and elegant toward the end of the 16th century in the act of painting a *Resurrection*.

Titian (Tiziano Vecellio), (1488/1490–1576)
*Portrait of Count Antonio di Porcia
and Brugnera*
Oil on canvas, 115 x 93 cm

The work was painted in Titian's mature period. It depicts a gentleman from Friuli next to a window giving onto a landscape, a composition style that the artist used in numerous official portraits. The penetrating and somewhat tense gaze of the young count contrasts with the prevalently dark tones in the rest of the painting, which unfortunately is not well preserved.

Paris Bordon (1500–1571)
The Lovers, circa 1525
Oil on canvas, 80.5 x 86 cm

Realised around 1525 by the painter from Treviso, the painting has been interpreted in a number of different ways. Some see it as an episode of prostitution, a recurrent theme in Venetian painting: a courtesan, watched from the shadows by her protector, receives a gift from her somewhat embarrassed client. But it has also been interpreted as representing a proposal of marriage: two young lovers, immersed in a suffused atmosphere à la Giorgione, are exchanging wedding vows.

Lorenzo Lotto (1480–1556)
Portrait of Laura da Pola, 1543–44
Oil on canvas, 91 x 76 cm

Laura's apparently subdued bearing contrasts sharply with the pomp of her velvet and embroidered dress and the ostentatious display of precious objects stating her status: the rings and ostrich plume fan with its gold chain. Acquired in 1859 through the mediatorship of King Vittorio Emanuele II together with the pendant with the portrait of Laura's husband, Febo da Brescia, the portrait was painted in 1543–44, perhaps on the occasion of the wedding of the two aristocrats from Treviso.

45

Room VIII

This is the first of the spacious neoclassical galleries known as the "Napoleonic Halls", created in 1809 by building a loft into the nave of the Medieval church of Santa Maria di Brera in order to accommodate the Royal Gallery as desired by Napoleon. Separated by Corinthian columns, the galleries were rebuilt after the Second World War under the direction of architect Piero Portaluppi, who embellished them with elegant marble. The current exhibition design is the result of Vittorio Gregotti's work in the 1990s, introducing the innovative cross-shaped roof windows, which are used to diffuse natural lighting in the galleries. Like the next two galleries, Room VIII contains large-format religious paintings from the Renaissance (late 14th and 15th centuries), originally from suppressed churches and convents in the capital and lands of the Most Serene Republic of Venice. The imposing large canvases are represented here by Michele da Verona's *Crucifixion*, originally in the refectory of the Veronese monastery of San Giorgio in Braida, and by two paintings from the Venetian Scuola Grande di San Marco: the celebrated *Saint Mark Preaching in Alexandria* by the Bellini brothers and *Saint Mark Baptising Anianus* by Giovanni Mansueti. The other works allow us to follow the development of the single-panel altarpiece, which replaced the former polyptychs. One example is *Saint Bernard and Angels* by Andrea Mantegna and helpers. However, the most widely explored subject are the *Holy Conversations*, groups of saints gathered around the Virgin in silent meditation. The gallery offers two extraordinary examples by Bartolomeo Montagna.

Cima da Conegliano (*circa* 1459 – *circa* 1517)
Saint Peter Martyr with Saints Nicholas of Bari and Benedict
Oil on panel, 330 x 216 cm

The important early 16th-century altarpiece from the Church of Corpus Domini in Venice represents one of the peaks of Giovan Battista Cima's oeuvre. The Dominican saint on a pedestal and the two figures on either side are clearly described in a Classical architectural setting, with a massive arch giving onto a luminous landscape under a blue sky with bright clouds.

Gentile (1429–1507) and Giovanni Bellini
(*circa* 1430–1516)
Saint Mark Preaching in Alexandria
Oil on canvas, 347 x 770 cm

The enormous canvas, commissioned
in 1504 to Gentile Bellini by the confraternity
of San Marco, was part of a series depicting
episodes from the life of the saint decorating
the Scuola Grande. Just back from
Constantinople, where he was summoned to
paint the portrait of Sultan Mehmed II,
Gentile is responsible for the composition
and the extraordinary oriental guise of the
city, populated with an incredible variety of
people and animals, and combining
accurate Arabic architecture with a mosque
clearly inspired by Saint Mark's Basilica in
Venice. Giovanni, who completed the work
after the death of his brother in 1507, is by all
accounts the author of the group of
onlookers in the foreground listening to
the saint's last sermon, and in particular
the people on the left side of the painting,
who include a number of members of
the confraternity. Women wearing long
white veils are seated on the ground at
centre, while dignitaries dressed in brightly
coloured clothing converse amongst
themselves on the right.

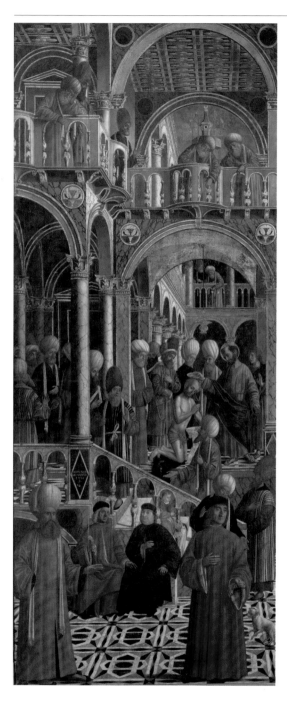

Giovanni Mansueti
(*circa* 1465–1526/27)
*Saint Mark
baptising Anianus*
Oil on canvas,
335 x 135 cm

This is another
canvas from the
cycle in the Scuola
Grande di San
Marco. The
Venetian artist
painted the
principal episode
in the middle
distance, among
a host of people
in picturesque
costumes, within
a multicoloured
architectural
setting with a
perspective
structure
embellished with
gold and so
complex as to
appear unreal.

Bartolomeo
Montagna (*circa*
1450–1523)
*Virgin and Child
Enthroned with
Saints Andrew,
Monica, Orsola and
Sigismund*, 1499
Oil on canvas,
410 x 260 cm

This beautiful
canvas was once
the altarpiece in the
Squarzi Chapel in
the Church of San
Michele in Vicenza.
The solemn figures
of the saints
and the mild Virgin
are set in a
very complex
architectural
structure, inspired
by Montagna's
studies of
Bramante's
architecture in
Lombardy.
The interplay of
light and shadow
is accented by the
openings in the
upper part of the
structure.

HIERONIMVS DE SOVANTVS XVLRA
M.....ANT O.D.XXV.

Room IX

The 16th century witnessed the triumph of artists gravitating around Venice. Governed by the Dogi, the city enjoyed a political stability that favoured the accumulation of great wealth through its sea trade and vast landholdings. The enlightened patronage of the Republic and of the rich merchants and aristocrats filled churches, palazzi and the *Scuole* of the confraternities with works of art. Most of the paintings in this room are the work of two exceptional protagonists of the "Venetian manner", at times rivals for the Republic's important commissions, Jacopo Tintoretto and Paolo Veronese. Their works exhibited here are true pillars in 16th-century Italian art. A fundamental point of reference for both of them – albeit to different degrees – was Titian, an internationally famous artist represented here with a panel from his late mature period, *Saint Jerome in Penitence*, characterised by an earthy chromatic scheme and multilayered brushwork. Jacopo Bassano and Lorenzo Lotto gravitated around the same artistic centre but exhibited radically different sensibilities. The former developed an original style of realistic genre painting with a very personal reinterpretation of Tintoretto's luministic effects, while Lotto, represented here with a *Pietà*, reveals a profoundly religious tension.

Tintoretto (Jacopo Robusti known as),
(1519–1594)
The Finding of the Body of Saint Mark
Oil on canvas, 396 x 400 cm

The large canvas, belonging to the cycle
from the Scuola Grande di San Marco,
was commissioned in 1562 by the physician
Tommaso Rangone, portrayed in the
centre of the scene.

In a spacious and scenographic
mausoleum, Saint Mark stands next to his
foreshortened body in a commanding pose,
interrupting the search for his body and
healing the frenzied demoniac.
The flickering artificial light effectively
highlights the vaults and tombs of the
unreal architecture and the over-
lengthened bodies of the protagonists in
the midst of their drama.

Paolo Veronese (Paolo Caliari known as),
(1528–1588)
Feast in the House of Simon, 1570
Oil on canvas, 275 x 710 cm

Created in 1570 for the refectory of the
Convent of San Sebastiano in Venice, the
large canvas is one of the most outstanding
interpretations of an "evangelical feast",
original scenes of banquettes that
Veronese set against architectural
backgrounds inspired by the villas built by
his contemporary Andrea Palladio. Here,
around the symmetrically arranged and
sumptuously laid tables at the house of the
Pharisee, mixed in among many vivacious
characters drawn from the common folk,
we see on the left the scene of the sinner
drying the feet of Christ, and Judas rising
from his chair on the right and observing
the scene with irritation. The bright colour
palette generally used by the painter has
been altered in some areas due to poorly
executed restoration work. In the *Last
Supper* from his late period on the opposite
wall, Veronese paints the loggia where
Christ is having his frugal meal with the
Apostles along a diagonal perspective line.

Lorenzo Lotto (1480–1556)
Pietà, 1538–45
Oil on canvas, 185 x 150 cm

Painted in the years 1538–45 for the
Dominican church of San Paolo in Treviso,
the work exhibits a personal interpretation
of the northern-European iconography of the
Pietà, alien to the Venetian repertoire.

The protagonists are arranged in a dramatic
and unstable pyramid that stands out against
the dark background: the dead body of the
Son in full light lying across the lap of the
elderly Virgin, who in turn is supported under
the arms by Saint John. The religious unrest
shaking the Catholic church at the time also
disturbed Lorenzo Lotto, a deeply religious
and non-conformist man and painter.

Jacopo Bassano
(Jacopo da Ponte),
(*circa* 1510–1592)
*Saint Roch and
the Plague Victims*
Oil on canvas,
350 x 210 cm

The large altarpiece
from the Church of
San Rocco in
Vicenza was
probably an *ex-voto*
for the end of the
plague that had
infested the city in
1575. Although well
versed in Venetian
pictorial culture, the
artist preferred to
work in the
provinces, focusing
on the rural world,
which he features
in his sacred works.
He interpreted
these subjects in
a style that
transmutes into
ceaseless
experimentation,
always maintaining,
however, a
straightforward
attention to reality.

Room X

This elongated space was redesigned in 2004 to accommodate the Jesi Collection. The desire to present the collection in its entirety for the first time – one of the broadest, most coherent and select anthologies of Italian art from the first half of the twentieth century, including 68 paintings and 12 sculptures – inevitably demanded a closely spaced layout, sacrificing the benefits of a more dilated arrangement. Emilio Jesi, who died in 1974, was a dedicated collector. In the 1930s and '40s and again in the post-war years, he assembled an exceptional collection of works. Guided by his passion for contemporary art, he frequented the leading art galleries of the period and sometimes dealt directly with the artists themselves, forging friendships as well as relations of patronage. In 1976 and again in 1984, his wife Maria acted to fulfil her husband's often expressed desire to make the most representative part of his collection available to the public by donating it to the Pinacoteca di Brera. The masterpieces of Futurism and Metaphysical painting constitute the principal nucleus of the gift, with artists of the calibre of Umberto Boccioni, Carlo Carrà, Mario Sironi, Giorgio Morandi and Filippo de Pisis. The sculptors Arturo Martini and Marino Marini are also well represented, with a number of important masterpieces. The Jesi Collection has marked a significant turning point in the development of the museum, which has now opened its doors to modern art and sculpture. Indeed, other works, acquired by the State, have been added to this room, such as a number of paintings done by Italian artists for the Parisian residence of the art dealer Léonce Rosenberg.

Umberto Boccioni (1882–1916)
Riot at the Gallery, 1910
Oil on canvas, 74 x 64 cm

In the Galleria Vittorio Emanuele II of Milan, illuminated by electric lamps, a curious crowd runs to gather around two women tearing at each other's hair in front of a café. The energy transmitted by the moving bodies and the artificial lights are an expression of the modern city, undergoing in the early 20th century a process of transformation exalted by the Futurist movement. Boccioni uses the divisionist (pointillist) painting technique, with a combined series of light dabs of colour that the eye reads as a prevalence of aggressive, violent tones.

Carlo Carrà (1881–1966)
The Metaphysical Muse, 1917
Oil on canvas, 90 x 66 cm

Along with two other nearby canvases, this
is one of the great masterpieces of
Metaphysical Art, which developed thanks
to the encounter between Carrà and
De Chirico in the military hospital in Ferrara,
a movement to which Morandi also adhered
for a brief period. A number of inanimate
objects belonging to the sphere of individual
imagery are arranged in a brightly lit room in
a perspective view: the muse, i.e., the chalky
mannequin dressed in tennis whites is
positioned in relation to a map of Istria, a
theatre of war precisely in 1917, and to a
colourful hexahedron in the background.

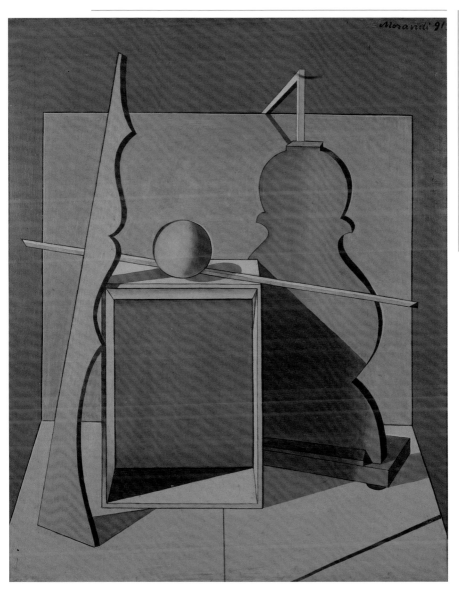

Giorgio Morandi (1890–1964)
Still-life, 1919
Oil on canvas, 56.5 x 47 cm

Among the best known paintings by the Bolognese artist – who is represented in the Jesi Collection with a full 13 works – this still-life aptly documents the leanness of his metaphysical expression. A rectangular box, a sphere, a rod and the contoured outline of a clock are arranged with geometrical rigour in full light on a slanting base. The staggered shadows, the black outlines and the limited range of browns contribute to the limpidness of the forms and to the impression of a balanced stillness.

Pablo Picasso (1881–1973)
Head of a Bull, 1942
Oil on canvas, 116 x 89 cm

Painted in Paris by the renowned Spanish
artist during the Second World War, this is
a famous still-life where the severed head
of a bull, evoking the bucrania of Greco-
Roman Classical era buildings, transforms
into a brutal metaphor for the horrors of
war. The still bleeding head sits on a table
covered with a white cloth in front of a
closed window. Spare brushstrokes in red
paint heighten the horror and pain of the
almost snarling skull.

Alberto Savinio (1891–1952)
Le gîte des promesses (*La cité des
promesses*)
Oil on canvas, 97 x 146 cm

This is one of the first paintings by Alberto
Savinio, writer, poet, essayist and brother of
Giorgio de Chirico. It was commissioned by
the Paris art merchant Léonce Rosenberg
to decorate one of the rooms in his new
apartment. A "transparent city", composed
of skewed geometrical constructions about
to topple down, floats on a raised platform
against a colourful sky.

Mario Sironi (1885–1961)
Urban Landscape with Wayfarer, 1929
Oil on panel, 70 x 67 cm

An urban landscape composed of buildings
in rationalist style, shadowy walls and
factories with smokestacks is dominated by
the expressionistic figure of a wayfarer,
isolated, looming and monumental.
The colour palette is limited to greys and
browns spread with full, almost gestural
brushwork. An exponent of the Novecento
movement, which was centred on a "return
to order" and to the figurative tradition,
Sironi briefly summarises the industrial
outskirts of the modern city.

Filippo de Pisis (1896–1956)
Bouquet of Flowers, 1930
Oil on canvas, 81 x 53 cm

De Pisis is represented in the Jesi
Collection with a full 15 paintings, which
encompass some thirty years of his career,
much of which was spent in Paris.
The large and varied bouquet of cut flowers
evoke De Pisis's botanical interests as a
teenager. The vase is placed in front of a
painting and there are two books behind it.
The symphony of vivid colours in this
sumptuous still-life brings to mind
Impressionist paintings, and particularly
those by Renoir.

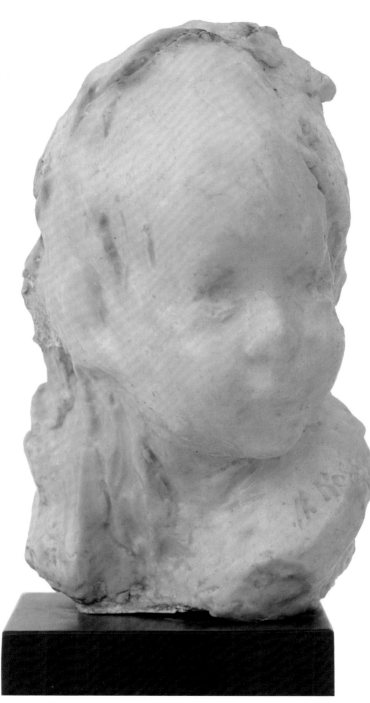

Medardo Rosso
(1858–1928)
L'enfant juif,
1892–93
Wax, height 25 cm

The sad child's face modelled in wax reveals the ability of this sculptor, who spent almost his entire career in Paris, to create portraits.
The inherent qualities of this material allow the figure to merge with the atmosphere, a characteristic shared with Impressionist painting. The light bathing the small head brings out its furtive expression. Next to it, the showcase also contains *Dame à la voilette* and *La petite rieuse.*

Arturo Martini
(1889–1947)
Drinker, 1928–29
Terracotta, height
150.5 cm

The figure of a man
drinking, a typical
subject in 19th and
early 20th-century
painting, is
rendered in
terracotta by
Martini in a neo-
primitive manner:
the slender youth
seated on a stump
and drinking from a
rustic bowl
elegantly evokes
the Classical world,
which is revisited
here with simple
and modern forms.
Other works on
display by this
sculptor, who was
self-taught but well
versed in both
ancient and modern
models, include the
two very different
versions of *Ophelia*,
one in terracotta
and the other, a
very recent
acquisition, in
plaster.

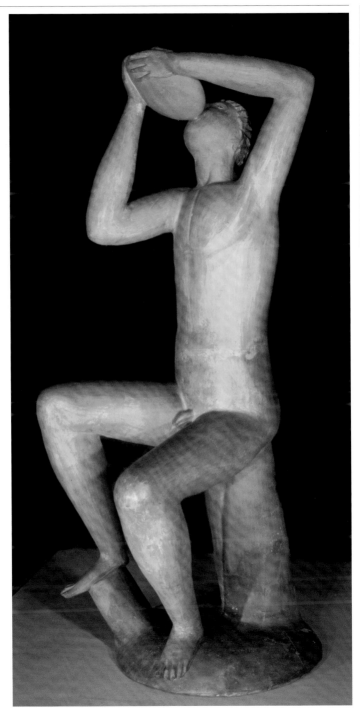

Room XI

The collection of Lamberto Vitali, a principal player on the Milan cultural scene in the post Second World War period, was bequeathed to the Pinacoteca in 1999 and 2000. It documents the eclectic interests of this autodidact, scholar and militant art critic. Installed in this room in 2004, the collection comprises a nucleus of some 80 art objects of extremely high quality: sculptures, jewellery, mosaics, and paintings in various techniques from different schools and periods. It includes an extraordinary archaeological section with such works as the Naqata vases from the 4th millennium BC, small Cycladic limestone idols, Greek ribbon diadems and Faiyum mummy portraits.

These objects attest to Vitali's taste for the primitive, which is also found in the "primitive" Medieval works of Italian figurative art, with gold-ground works such as the altarpiece of *Saint Louis of Toulouse* by the Master of San Martino. A reflection of Vitali's pioneering studies of the Macchiaioli are the *Portrait of Brother Ettore as a Boy* by Silvestro Lega and the *Lady Outdoors* by Giovanni Fattori. A "primitive" interpretation of the forms of the 20th century is expressed in *L'enfant gras* by Modigliani and the important paintings by Giorgio Morandi, whose entire catalogue was curated by Vitali. To make clear the collector's eclectic tastes, the exhibition is not placed in chronological order but arranged instead to suggest various combinations and links between the different objects.

Art of Roman Egypt
Mummy Portrait of a Woman, circa 160 AD
Encaustic painting on wood, 39 x 16 cm

The beautiful portrait, painted when the woman was alive, was enclosed in the mummy wrappings over the face of the deceased. In spite of the faded colours, it still transmits the freshness of the face of a young woman with olive skin and a penetrating gaze, accentuated by thick eyebrows and embellished with jewels. Along with two other portraits on panels, this work originates in the Faiyum area of Egypt, west of the Nile valley. Encaustic painting uses pigments added to heated beeswax.

Amedeo Modigliani (1884–1920)
L'enfant gras, 1915
Oil on canvas, 45.5 x 37.5 cm

The painting once belonged to Paul Guillaume, a friend and for years the only buyer of the work of the artist from Leghorn. Modigliani was an isolated but original voice in the choir of early 20th century Parisian art. The girl's face is summarised in the geometrical forms of the oval face and typically long neck, outlined with black lines and filled with flat, expressionist colour fields.
The reddish skin contrasts with the brown of the groomed hair.

Cycladic Art
Small Female Idol,
2500–2100 BC
White marble,
16.2 x 6 x 3.5 cm

This small marble statue of a female figure is a sacred artistic expression associated with the religion of the Cycladic civilisation, which developed on a group of islands (Cyclades) in the Aegean Sea from approximately 3000 to 2000 BC. The essentially formed statue of a nude woman standing with folded arms in a hieratic attitude represents the Mother Goddess, symbol of fertility. It was quite probably originally found in a tomb, like the other small Cycladic idols in Parian or Naxos marble that are part of this collection.

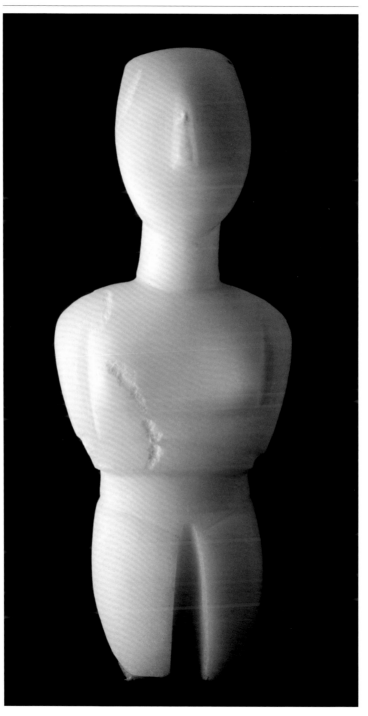

Rooms XII-XIII

The space in which the chapel of San Giuseppe of the Franciscan church of Santa Maria della Pace in Milan had been reproduced was reworked in 2004. The frescoes, which were brought to the Pinacoteca in the 19th century following Napoleon's suppression of the churches, were installed here by the superintendent Ettore Modigliani in 1924, following plans by Piero Portaluppi. The *Stories of the Virgin and Joseph*, painted by the Milanese painter Bernardino Luini, evoke the renewed devotion to Mary, and hence also to her spouse, sparked by the Franciscan Amadeites, who were based in the convent adjacent to the church. In the small room leading to the chapel there are two paintings on panels from the church. These are portions of a fragmented polyptych by the painters Giovanni Agostino da Lodi and Marco d'Oggiono. Agostino is largely responsible for the composition in the *Baptism of Christ* and the *Adoration of the Magi*, while the figure of Christ in the *Baptism* and the faces of Mary and Jesus in the *Adoration* are the work of Leonardo's apprentice d'Oggiono. Together with Luini's frescoes, they document the orientation of painting in French-dominated Milan in the early decades of the 16th century.

The Chapel of San Giuseppe.

Bernardino Luini
(1480/82–1532)
*Saint Joseph
chosen as the
Spouse of the Virgin*
Fresco transferred
onto canvas,
315 x 178 cm

Set in a complex
architecture
reminiscent of
Bramante, the
painting above the
altar depicts three
different scenes
from the same
episode, according
to a story contained
only in the
Apocalypsis Nova
written by Amadeo
Mendez da Silva:
in the foreground,
Saint Joseph with
his flowering staff is
portrayed among
the spurned suitors;
to the left, in the
background, the
angel that appeared
to Joseph in a
dream; and the
newly betrothed in
prayer.

Giovanni Agostino da Lodi (documented between the end of the 15th century and *circa* 1520) and Marco d'Oggiono (documented between 1475 and 1524)
Adoration of the Magi
Oil on panel, 176 x 116 cm

The *Adoration of the Magi* and the *Baptism of Christ* are traditionally considered to be parts of the polyptych commissioned by the former bishop of Bobbio, Battista Bagarotti, for the main altar of Santa Maria della Pace. The two panels, dating to the 1510s, are probably part of an altarpiece, but it is not known whether they were painted by the two artists working together or if Marco took over from Giovanni.

Room XIV

The imposing statue of *Napoleon as Mars the Pacifier* by Canova, on loan from the Brera Academy of Fine Arts after its recent restoration (2008–09), underscores the strong link between the emperor and the museum's origins. Located in the centre of the large gallery dedicated to 16th-century works produced in the flourishing cities on the mainland of the Veneto region, the statue is a commanding view from the museum entrance and constitutes a visual pivot point for the visitor. Of more clearly Venetian style are the sumptuously coloured paintings by Paris Bordon of Treviso, Bonifacio de' Pitati of Verona, and Giovanni Cariani, who was active mainly in Bergamo. In the important works of Romanino, Moretto and Savoldo (all from Brescia), Moroni (Bergamo) and Lotto (during his stay in Bergamo), the Venetian pictorial influence joins with the naturalism of the Lombard tradition, expressed through the depiction of well defined gestures and sentiments and attention to light and the realism. The young Merisi (Caravaggio) would absorb these works before moving on to Rome. The *Pala di Pesaro*, the most important public work by Giovan Gerolamo Savoldo, is outstanding for its dimensions and quality: the realistic and monumental figures of the two narrative orders are harmoniously set between earth and heaven.

Antonio Canova (1757–1822) *Napoleon as Mars the Pacifier*, 1808 Plaster, height 430 cm Temporary loan from the Brera Fine Arts Academy of Milan

The colossal statue, weighing approximately one and a half tons, reproduces the iconography of the marble statue of Napoleon sculpted a few years earlier. The head, an idealised rendition of Napoleon's actual head, is upon a statue in ancient style characterised by heroic nudity, with his chlamys draped over his raised left arm, which grips the regal sceptre. As in the bronze statue in the centre of the palazzo's courtyard of honour, a winged victory should be perched on top of the sceptre.

NIL MAIVS GENERATVR IPSO
NEC VIGET QVICQVAM SIMILE AVT SECVNDVM
HORAT

Jacopo Palma
the Elder (Jacopo
Negretti known as),
(*circa* 1480–1528)
*Adoration of the
Magi with Saint
Helena*, 1525–26
Oil on canvas,
470 x 260 cm

Recently restored
to its original
chromatic
brilliance, the large
canvas, painted
in the artist's
mature period,
was originally found
in the Venetian
church of
Sant'Elena in Isola.
Indeed, in the
foreground of the
atmospheric
landscape, in
addition to the
traditional
iconography of the
adoring Magi,
we see Helena,
mother of the
Roman emperor
Constantine,
discovering the
True Cross.

Giovanni Gerolamo
Savoldo (*circa* 1480
– *post* 1548)
*Virgin and Child in
Glory with Angels
and Saints* (*Pala
di Pesaro*), 1524–26
Oil on panel,
511.7 x 311.6 cm

The grandiose
structure for the
altar was created in
Venice in 1524–26
for the now
destroyed church
of the Dominican
convent in Pesaro.
The altarpiece was
complemented with
a predella and
frieze with *Dead
Christ*. It has been
at Brera since 1811
and recently
underwent
restoration work
completed in 2005.
According to the
narrative scheme
of Titian's and
Raphael's
altarpieces, the
Virgin with Child
and the two angels
playing instruments
stand out on high
against the
luminous disk of
cherubs, while
below, in the
dawning light, the
fully human saints
Peter, Dominic,
Paul and Jerome
stand overlooking
Venice from the
Fondamenta Nuove.

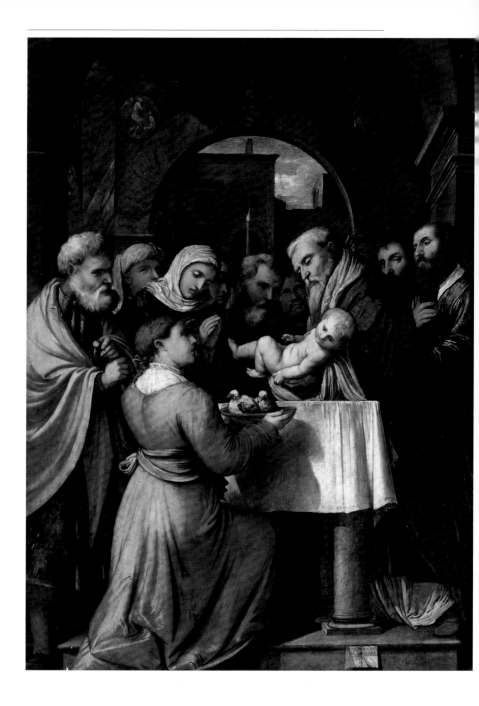

Romanino (Gerolamo de' Romani known as),
(1484/1487–1560)
Presentation of Jesus in the Temple, 1529
Oil on panel, 188 x 144 cm

The artist was well aware of the style of
another painter from Brescia, Moretto,
when he painted this panel in 1529. It
illustrates the Biblical episode of the
presentation of Jesus in the temple and the
offering of turtledoves and pigeons within a
Classical setting. Intent on the rite, the
people nearly fill the space. The soft light
illuminates their expressive faces in the
semi-darkness, almost true portraits.

Giovan Battista Moroni (1520/24–1578)
*Madonna and Child with the Saints Catherine
and Francis and a Donor, circa* 1550
Oil on canvas, 102 x 110 cm

Created for private worship as suggested
by its dimensions, compositional style
and the presence of the donor, the work
was painted circa 1550 by Moroni, from
Bergamo, who was specialised in
portraiture. The patron, separated from the
holy group by a marble balustrade, is
depicted praying with hands together.
The Virgin and Saint Catherine of Alexandria
are dressed in the manner of 16th century
ladies. The Child sits on an elegant cushion
and offers a rose to the saint.

81

Room XV

The last of the Napoleonic Halls houses paintings, mainly of large-format, created in Milan or Lombardy in the final decades of the 15th century, when the lord of the city and the Sforza Duchy was Ludovico il Moro, and in the first half of the 16th century, initially under French dominion and subsequently with the Sforzas restored to power under the Spanish protectorate. Late 15th-century Lombard Renaissance painting was strongly influenced by two extremely famous artists active in the Milanese court: Donato Bramante and Leonardo da Vinci. In the frescoes from the Church of Santa Maria di Brera Vincenzo Foppa of Brescia proposed architecture inspired by Bramante. Bramantino developed his own original Classical and monumental style, while the Master of the Pala Sforzesca, who got his name from the very painting found here in the museum, slavishly reproduced Leonardo's models. There are also many works by Ambrogio Bergognone, who created frescoes and altarpieces for the Chartreuse of Pavia and for the principal churches of Milan, and by Gaudenzio Ferrari of Valsesia, with the fresco decorations of a chapel in Santa Maria della Pace, which is also the origin of the *Annunciation*, recently reattributed to Bernardo Zenale. Of the Leonardesque Marco d'Oggiono there are two panels depicting relatively uncommon topics, *The Three Archangels* and the *Assumption of the Magdalene*.

Vincenzo Foppa (*circa* 1427/1430 – 1515/1516) *Polyptych of the Graces, circa* 1500 Tempera and oil on panel, 420 x 300 cm

One of the pillars in the painter's oeuvre, the polyptych is from the main altar of the Franciscan church of Santa Maria delle Grazie in Bergamo and dates to *circa* 1500. In a profusion of gold and elaborate fabrics, it shows an attempt to unify the architecture of the two orders of saints in the side panels. The solemn figures are characterised by greyish-silver skin tones and the humanity of their gestures is typical of the Lombard figurative culture of the time.

Master of the Pala Sforzesca (active in
Lombardy between 1490 and *circa* 1520)
Pala Sforzesca, circa 1494
Tempera on panel, 230 x 165 cm

This extremely famous altarpiece was
realised for the Church of Sant'Ambrogio ad
Nemus in Milan by an unknown artist.
Commissioned by Ludovico Sforza
("The Moor"), whom we see portrayed with
his family among the Doctors of the Church
and next to the Madonna and Child, the work
celebrates the Milanese dynasty. The group
in the centre is inspired by Leonardo,
hardened by the strong lines of the design.
The clothing, jewellery and hair of the ducal
couple precisely reproduce the prevailing
fashions of the times in the Sforza court.

Bramantino (Bartolomeo Suardi known as),
(*circa* 1465–1530)
Crucifixion
Oil on canvas, 372 x 270 cm

This unsettling painting, created in the first decade of the 16th century by Bramante's apprentice, who had already developed a style of his own, has been in the Brera collections since 1806. In front of the cross, in the foreground, the people seem frozen in rigid poses; on either side of Christ an angel and a demon kneel on floating clouds against the background of an ideal Jerusalem with simplified geometrical architecture.

Gaudenzio Ferrari (*circa* 1475/1480–1546)
Martyrdom of Saint Catherine of Alexandria
Oil on panel, 334 x 210 cm

The large panel, characterised by brilliant
colours, comes from the Franciscan church
of Sant'Angelo in Milan. Commissioned by
the Gallarati family around 1540, when
Gaudenzio was at the height of his career,
it presents a rather theatrical and unusual
iconography of the martyrdom of the saint.
She is pictured half nude in near ecstasy
between the breaking wheels driven by
cruel muscle men, while above an angel
bursts onto the scene to halt the torture.

Marco d'Oggiono (*circa* 1475–1524)
The Three Archangels
Oil on panel, 255 x 190 cm

This work was on the altar dedicated to
archangel Michael in the Milanese church
of Santa Marta, which was officiated in the
early decades of the 16th century by
Augustinian nuns. The non-ritual subject,
Michael driving out the demon, was inspired
by the vision of Amadeo Mendez da Silva
recounted in *Apocalypsis Nova*, in which
the cult of the angels is a central theme.
The archangels and the landscape reflect
the influence of Leonardo.

Room XVIII

The interior design of the room dates back to 1950. Since 2006 it has housed the restoration workshop, equipped with all the necessary technology and tools. The transparent box was designed and built in order to make it possible to restore large-format panels that cannot be removed from the museum, and in particular, the *Pala di Pesaro* by Giovan Gerolomo Savoldo (Room XIV). The works in the room document the 16th-century schools of painting in cities such as Cremona or Lodi, which gravitated around Milan to some extent while also maintaining close ties with Venice. One of the more successful botteghe in Lodi was that owned by the Piazza family, here represented by the altarpiece with the *Baptism of Christ* by Callisto Piazza. The artists from Cremona are better documented, with some of them achieving truly noteworthy results. They include the highly talented Sofonisba Anguissola, Camillo Boccaccino and the Campi brothers. Vincenzo Campi is represented with four canvases attesting to the grand achievements of Italian genre painting at the end of the 16th century. Equally important are the two large altarpieces by Giulio and Antonio Campi, reflecting the Italian Mannerist figurative culture that would influence all of European art in the late sixteenth century.

Vincenzo Campi (1536–1591)
Fruit Seller, circa 1590
Oil on canvas, 143 x 213 cm

Together with the *Fish Monger*, the *Poultry Seller* and the *Kitchen* displayed alongside it, the *Fruit Seller* is part of a series of four canvases painted *circa* 1590, with subjects that may allude to the four seasons or elements. They come originally from the guesthouse of the convent of the Hieronymite monks of San Sigismondo in Cremona. A lively narrator of his later genre works, Vincenzo Campi describes with scientific exactitude the fruits laid out in baskets, tubs and ceramic plates and hawked by the young grocer whose lap is full of peaches.

Callisto Piazza
(*circa* 1500–1562)
Baptism of Christ
Oil on canvas,
295 x 255 cm

In the mid-16th
century, the painter
from Lodi
reproduced with
some variants the
illustrious model of
Gaudenzio Ferrari's
altarpiece for the
Milanese church of
Santa Maria presso
San Celso. Echoes
of Leonardo's
influence are seen
in the atmospheric
landscape in the
background and the
softly rendered
flesh of the human
figures, in spite of
their vigorous
physiques. The
saturated colours
reveal the influence
of the Venetia
school of painting.

Giovanni Ambrogio
Figino (1553–1608)
*Portrait of Lucio
Foppa*
Oil on panel,
196 x 99 cm

The elegant Lucio
Foppa is portrayed
in full figure, as was
customary in the
official portraiture
of the time. He is
wearing his armour
while his helmet
with its crest and
his sword are laid
on the table. The
Milanese painter
reproduces with
great precision an
armour produced at
the end of the 16th
century in the
Milanese
workshops.

91

Room XIX

R ecently redesigned with the addition of important paintings from internal storage, the room offers a rich panorama of Milanese and Lombard painting in the decades around the turn of the 16th century, marked by the work of Vincenzo Foppa, Ambrogio Bergognone, Leonardo da Vinci, Bernardo Zenale and Bernardino Luini. The works are mostly small or medium panels, prevalently Madonnas and Child painted for the purposes of private devotion.

A number of painters were oriented toward Leonardo and his achievements, particularly in the study of the human figure. These include his direct appentices, such as Boltraffio and Marco d'Oggiono and others who felt his influence through different channels, such as Giampietrino and Cesare da Sesto.

The beautiful portraits by Boltraffio and Andrea Solario are also within the Leonardesque ambit, paired with the extraordinary *Christ Derided*, work of the young Giovanni Antonio Bazzi, known as Sodoma, on loan to the Pinacoteca from a generous collector. Among the altarpieces, is outstanding the *Pala Busti*, recently attributed to Bernardo Zenale and dating to 1515–18. In this work, Zenale appears very close to Bernardino Luini in style, the latter documented here with the famous *Madonna of the Rose Garden* and *Ham's Scorn*.

In 1997 the museum acquired a panel with Saint John the Baptist, the side panel of a polyptych, by Donato de' Bardi, a painter from Pavia active in the first half of the 15th century, especially in Liguria and with few works in museums.

Bergognone (Ambrogio da Fossano known as), (1451/1456–1525)
Virgin and Child, Saint Catherine of Siena and a Carthusian Monk
Tempera on panel, 46 x 40.5 cm

The small panel was created for the private devotion of a Carthusian monk at the Chartreuse of Pavia, where the young Bergognone realised frescoes and altarpieces from 1486 to 1494.
The praying monk may be Stefano Maconi, who was prior in the early 15th century and a point of reference for his community. A landscape is visible in the upper part of the painting. The flesh tones and poses of the figures reveal the influence of Vincenzo Foppa.

Bernardo Zenale (*circa* 1460–1526)
Madonna and Child and two Musical Angels
Oil on panel, 57 x 41 cm

The small devotional panel, long hidden
in storage, dates to the first decade of
the 16th century, when the artist from
Treviglio, studying not only the works
of Vincenzo Foppa and Bergognone,
was also touched by the influence of
Leonardo da Vinci.
The two angels seated on pillows on
the windowsill are almost separated from
the protagonists, the nursing Virgin and
Child. Jesus is absorbed in playing with his
long coral necklace.

Andrea Solario (*circa* 1465–1524)
Madonna and Child with the Saints Joseph and Simeon, 1495
Tempera and oil on panel transferred to canvas, 102 x 87 cm

The small altarpiece with life-size figures comes from the Church of San Pietro Martire on the island of Murano. It dates to the year 1495, when Solario moved to Venice, where his brother Cristoforo was one of the major sculptors of his time. The painting reveals the bountiful encounter between the style of Leonardo da Vinci, expressed most notably in the figure of the Virgin, and the brilliant colours proper to Venetian painting. The strongly individualised faces of the saint and prophet show the influence of northern-European painting.

Rooms XX-XXI

The first room includes small format paintings by artists active in the courts of Lombardy and Emilia-Romagna who introduced original variants to the Renaissance figurative language during the 15th century. In the courts of the Este family in Ferrara particularly, the mid-15th century witnessed the development of a refined school of painting that succeeded in harmonising the late Gothic heritage of elegance and extreme naturalism with the latest in figurative humanism, inspired strongly by Leon Battista Alberti during his sojourn in the city. The leaders of this movement were Cosmè Tura, Francesco del Cossa and Ercole de' Roberti, brought together in the early 1470s for the decoration of the Salone dei Mesi in Palazzo Schifanoia.

Room XXI was set up starting in 1991-1992 with the large, late 15th-century polyptychs from The Marches, which came to the museum disassembled in the early years of the Pinacoteca. In 2010, after the show dedicated to Carlo Crivelli, the exhibition was redesigned to create a more articulate context for the restored works of the master, who was Venetian by origin but active mainly in The Marches, adding also the works by the great Luca Signorelli done in the same region. In the cities along the Adriatic coast and further inland, the seats of small landed seigniories, the traditional late Gothic polyptych with gold ground encountered the novelties of Renaissance art, resulting in a flourishing and very original art form especially in the Montefeltro court of Urbino.

Francesco del Cossa (*circa* 1436–1478) *Saint John the Baptist*, 1473 Tempera on panel, 112 x 55 cm

Along with its neighbour, a panel depicting Saint Peter, this work was part of the Griffoni Polyptych in the Basilica di San Petronio in Bologna. Dedicated to the sermoniser Vincenzo Ferrer and painted in 1473, it was a grandiose work divided in two registers, complemented with a predella painted by Ercole de' Roberti. The pillar behind the saint, the rock serving as a pedestal, and the chain with coral and rock crystal pendants are repeated in the different panels to give unity to the whole. The oneiric figure and imaginary landscape are described in such minute detail as to appear real.

97

Fra' Carnevale (Bartolomeo di Giovanni Corradini known as), (documented between 1445 and 1484)
Saint Peter, 1460-1465
Tempera on panel, 140 x 48 cm

This is one of the surviving panels of a polyptych that may have been created for the town of Cagli in The Marches. It was painted by Fra' Carnevale, a friar from Urbino, who was a disciple of Filippo Lippi in Florence and credited by Giorgio Vasari in his *Lives of the Artists* as being one of the early teachers of the architect Donato Bramante. One noteworthy feature of the painting is that it still conserves a portion of the original Gothic arcaded frame. Appearing almost as a statue, painted in a foreshortened view in front of a niche, dressed up in fabrics with strong chiaroscuro contrasts and his face creased by wrinkles, the expressive saint appears completely lost in thought.

Giovanni Angelo d'Antonio (documented between 1443 and 1481)
Gualdo Tadino Polyptych, 1462
Tempera on panel. Lower register: central panel, 132 x 60 cm; side panels, 118 x 42 cm. Upper register: central panel 190 x 60 cm; side panels, 154 x 42 cm.

On loan from the Museo Poldi Pezzoli, the work derives from the joining of two different polyptychs in the 20th century. The luministic painting style and careful rendering of space of this painter from The Marches greatly influenced Carlo Crivelli, who was struck by the simplified forms of the faces and the endearing signs of tenderness, such as the intertwined hands of the Virgin and Jesus at the centre of the lower register.

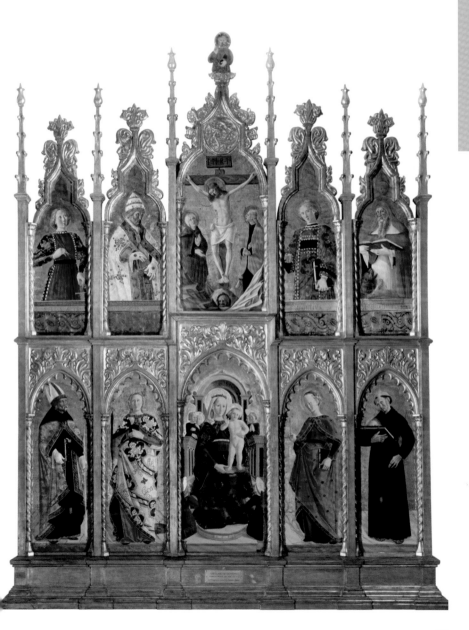

Carlo Crivelli (*circa* 1430–1494/1495)
Camerino Triptych, 1482
Tempera on panel. Central panel,
190 x 78 cm; side panels, 170 x 60 cm;
predelle, 26 x 62 cm

This triptych was located on the main altar
of the Church of San Domenico in Camerino
and is the first work done by the painter for
the city ruled by the Varano family. It was
originally a very elaborate work, with
predelle and also three large upper panels,
now in foreign museums. Restored in 2008,
this masterpiece is characterised by a
sumptuous profusion of details, by the gold
grounds made to imitate various fabrics,
and by applied elements or portions in
relief, such as the keys carried by Saint
Peter, who is dressed in elegant papal
vestments. The marble base is decorated
with fruits, animal skulls and sculptures,
maintaining a constant tension between the
real and the fictitious.

Carlo Crivelli (*circa* 1430–1494/1495) *Madonna of the Candeletta* Tempera and oil on panel, 219 x 74.5 cm

This has always been one of the best loved paintings in the museum. It once was the central panel in the huge polyptych, commissioned in 1488, that decorated the main altar of the cathedral in Camerino. The special allure of the image derives not only from the artist's extraordinary technical skill, but also from the balance between the sophisticated elegance of the forms, stirring realism of detail, an almost late-Gothic decorative richness, and the bold placement of the throne under the fruited pergola.

Luca Signorelli (*circa* 1445–1523) *Flagellation*, 1480–83 Tempera on panel, 84 x 60 cm each

With the *Virgin and Child* exhibited next to it, this work served as the two sides of a banner. It was painted at a time when Signorelli was closely attuned to the work of Piero della Francesca. Created for the confraternity of the Raccomandati of Santa Maria del Mercato in Fabriano, the banner reflects, in the two very different images, the activities of the fraternity brothers, who dedicated themselves to helping abandoned children and handling penitential procedures. The nervous and supple figures of the flagellators move within the space defined by the column to which Christ is bound and against a background representing ancient bas-reliefs.

Room XXII

Particularly interesting in this room, which houses one of the masterpieces of the Ferrara painter Ercole de' Roberti, is the development of painting in Ferrara, and in Romagna generally, in the 15th and early 16th centuries. In the court of Alfonso I d'Este, the prevailing figurative orientation was toward the Veneto region. Painters of the calibre of Mazzolino, Ortolano, Garofalo and particularly Dosso Dossi experimented with Venetian colourism, often joining it – to varying degrees depending on individual inclination – with the dominant Raphaelesque models that were circulating at the time in the form of engravings. Florence, Rome and Venice were unquestionably the leading centres of innovation in the figurative arts in those years. In Romagna, on the other hand, divided up among small autonomous seigniories, there were as many artistic orientations as there were political allegiances. In Ravenna, as we see in the works of Niccolò Rondinelli and the Zaganelli brothers, Venice exerted a powerful influence. In the works of Marco Palmezzano from Forlì, this influence was intermixed with the perspective culture of Melozzo da Forlì, with whom he had worked. Lastly, the widespread knowledge of Flemish painting led to the introduction of technical solutions and iconographic inventions marked by a subtle pathos.

Ercole de' Roberti (*circa* 1450–1496) *Madonna Enthroned with Saints (Pala Portuense)*, 1479–81 Oil on canvas, 323 x 240 cm

This masterpiece was created in Bologna. The protagonists are arranged in a pyramid structure framed within grandiose Renaissance architecture, accommodating the great marble throne and canopy and giving onto an open landscape. Seen between the small columns supporting the platform, the stormy sea refers to the near death by shipwreck of Pietro degli Onesti, pictured to the right, founder of the Canons Regular of the Lateran. He built the Ravenna church Santa Maria in Porto.

Niccolò Rondinelli (documented between 1495 and 1502)
Saint John the Apostle appearing to Galla Placidia
Oil on panel, 175 x 175 cm

With the empress Galla Placidia kneeling before Saint John the Apostle, the painting is strongly associated with the Ravenna church dedicated to the saint which is the source of the panel. The empress had the church built in the 5th century after she survived a shipwreck: it was to have contained one of the saint's relics, who had appeared to her and left her with a slipper. A striking effect is the painting within the painting, showing the Madonna and Child on the apsidal altar illuminated in bright daylight.

Marco Palmezzano (1459/1463-1539)
Crowning of the Virgin with Saint Francis and Benedict, 1494-1496
Oil on panel, 160 x 125 cm

Originally in the Church of the Osservanti in Cotignola, the altarpiece by this painter from Forlì is characterised by its bright, glossy colour palette and the influence of the Venetian painting style. The crowning of Mary takes place within a monumental tiered architectural setting, with the imposing figures of the main group, the saints and the musical angels placed on different levels.

Dosso Dossi
(Giovanni di Niccolò
Luteri known as),
(*circa* 1490–1542)
Saint Sebastian,
1527
Oil on panel,
182 x 95 cm

The panel by the
Emilian artist was
originally in the
church of the
Santissima
Annunziata in
Cremona.
The supple body
of the martyr,
accentuated by
the curves of the
beautiful green
cape, is in a forced
pose reflecting
the artist's
interpretation of
Raphael's mature
style, filtered down
through his
apprentices.
Dossi highlights in
the Giorgionesque
shadows the tragic
expression on
the saint's face
and the weapons
abandoned next
to him.

Garofalo (Benvenuto
Tisi known as),
circa 1476–1559)
*Mourning for Dead
Christ* or *Christ
Deposed*, 1527
Oil on panel,
300 x 166 cm

Originally on the
main altar of the
Church of
Sant'Antonio in
Polesine in Ferrara,
the altarpiece
effectively
exemplifies the
figurative choices
of this painter from
Ferrara. The glossy
and skilfully
juxtaposed colours
reflect the influence
of Venetian
colourism, of
Giorgione in
particular, while the
monumental figures
gathered around
Christ's body in the
foreground reflect
the influence of
Raphael and artists
from central Italy,
whom Garofalo
studied during his
sojourn in Rome.

Room XXIII

The room is almost entirely occupied by the first of two viewable storerooms, created in 1982 along the path through the Pinacoteca: paintings that cannot be put on display or need for conservation are hung on sliding steel racks. This solution allows them to be kept in climate-controlled environment while still being easily accessed by scholars. The few paintings that are displayed on the walls are works of maximum importance by Emilian artists in the early 16th century: the solemn *Annunciation* by Francesco Francia of Bologna, painted in 1505 in the court of Isabella d'Este Gonzaga in Mantua; and two rare early works by Correggio, a very important painter working in Parma in the first three decades of the 16th century.

Correggio (Antonio Allegri known as), (*circa* 1489–1534), *Nativity with Saint Elisabeth and Infant Saint John the Baptist*, 1512–13 Oil on panel, 79 x 100 cm

This small panel for a private patron was painted by Correggio in his early career when he was living in Mantua. The outdoor, northern scene shows a hut built upon Classical ruins. The sleeping Saint Joseph and Saint Elisabeth viewed in profile reflect the influence of Mantegna, while the tender Madonna instead evokes the gentle female figures of Lorenzo Costa of Bologna.

Correggio (Antonio Allegri known as), (*circa* 1489–1534)
Adoration of the Magi, 1516–17
Oil on canvas, 84 x 108 cm

Another work from Correggio's youth that comes from the collection of Cardinal Monti, donated in 1650 to the archbishop of Milan and entering the Brera collections in 1895. The scene is rich in detail and filled with secondary characters, set outdoors and bathed in an atmospheric light of Leonardesque derivation, which envelopes the figures and blurs their outlines. The main group is placed to the left and arranged in different planes by means of the expedient of the ruined colonnade.

Room XXIV

The room was created joining the three smaller rooms that accommodated separately the works of Piero della Francesca, Raphael and Bramante (following Piero Portaluppi's exhibition design of 1950). The new arrangement for the three crowning masterpieces of the Pinacoteca was the initiative of Carlo Bertelli, with designs by the architects Gregotti and Citterio. It was realised in 1983 for the occasion of the five hundredth anniversary of the birth of Raphael. The three artists were all associated in some way with the ducal court in Urbino: Raphael was born there and both he and Bramante began their training there, while the city was the fulcrum of an important phase in the career of Piero della Francesca. The three extraordinary masterpieces on panels are isolated on different walls of the room, illuminated by a carefully designed lighting system that integrates and balances overhead, natural and suffused lighting, and enhanced by the light colour of the floor. The work by Piero della Francesca is illuminated via the French doors on the balcony, mimicking the illumination within the large altarpiece itself, which comes through a window intuited to the left and reflects off the armour of condottiero Federico. Restoration work, which also produced a wealth of knowledge, was performed recently on Piero's *Pala Montefeltro* (in 1980–82) and on Raphael's *Marriage of the Virgin* (in 2008–09).

Donato Bramante (Donato di Pascuccio d'Antonio known as), (1444–1514) *Christ at the Column* Tempera and oil on panel, 93.7 x 62.5 cm

The only known painting on panel by Bramante, this work arrived at Brera in 1915 from the Chiaravalle Abbey. In this powerful image created shortly after 1490, Bramante combines the spatial illusionism he learned in Urbino with Leonardo da Vinci's studies of anatomy and ability to convey emotions in expressions and gestures. The light highlights realistic details on the sculptural nude, such as the tensed muscles, the network of veins and the clear tears running down the cheeks of Christ's tragic face.

Piero della Francesca (1413–1492)
Pala Montefeltro
Oil and tempera on panel, 251 x 172 cm

A crowning work in the history of Italian
art painted by the Tuscan artist prior to
1474, the panel came to Brera in 1811 from
the Church of San Bernardino in Urbino.
The Holy Conversation is set in a
Renaissance-style church with the
Madonna and Child surrounded by saints
and angels. Federico da Montefeltro,
lord of Urbino, is pictured kneeling in
the foreground. The daylight accentuates
the forms of the solemn and motionless
figures, bringing out the most minute
details. The extraordinary effects of light
and shadow and rich texture are achieved
via thin and transparent layers of oil paint.
The ostrich egg hanging from the clamshell
in the apse alludes to Mary's purity
and fertility.

Raphael (Raffaello Sanzio), (1483–1520)
Marriage of the Virgin, 1504
Oil on panel, 170 x 118 cm

Signed and dated on the arch that girds
the radially symmetrical temple, this is the
masterpiece of the painter'a early career,
created for the Albizzini chapel in the Church
of San Francesco in Città di Castello. The
rite takes place in the foreground in the
presence of Mary's companions and
former suitors, thwarted by the miraculous
blossoming of Joseph's staff. The piazza
radiates outwards from the vanishing point
located in the door to the Classical temple,
which looks out upon the soft Umbrian
countryside. The frame with its Neoclassical
ornamentation is an extraordinary work in
itself, crafted before the end of 1810, shortly
after the work was received by Brera.

117

Room XXVII

The layout of the room was designed in 1950. It houses precious works, some of large format, realised in the first half of the 16th century by painters from central Italy, mainly from Tuscany and The Marches. Other works were added in the 1990s, specifically the large altarpiece with *Lamentation over the Dead Christ* by the Florentine Francesco Salviati, a work recovered from the Church of the Rosario in Viggiù, Province of Varese, where it had been deposited in the nineteenth century. The fruitful season in the arts that unites these works is Mannerism, which developed in Italy and Europe during the long political, religious and cultural crisis following the Sack of Rome in 1527. The figurative models of the great masters Raphael and Michelangelo were revisited by their apprentices and other artists who developed in Rome. They took poses, gestures and expressions to an extreme and experimented with design to create extraordinarily powerful images, often rich in artifice and Mannerist elegance. The room is dominated by the imposing panel by the Urbino architect and painter Girolamo Genga, a cultured and original re-elaboration of major figurative influences gained during his Roman sojourn.

Bronzino (Agnolo di Cosimo known as), (1503–1572) *Portrait of Andrea Doria as Neptune*, 1531–33 Oil on canvas, 115 x 53 cm

The allegorical portrait by the famous Florentine painter was commissioned by Paolo Giovio, a collector from Como, for his gallery of portraits of illustrious people. The Genoese admiral is celebrated in a portrayal as the god of the sea, bare-chested and grasping his trident. Bronzino was inspired by Michelangelo's sculpture of Moses, and the crisp and clear lines of the design underscore Doria's austere composure.

Girolamo Genga
(*circa* 1476–1551)
*Disputation over
the Immaculate
Conception*,
1516–18
Oil on panel,
438 x 290 cm

The work was once
the central panel of
a large altarpiece
decorating the main
altar of the Church
of Sant'Agostino in
Cesena. The
balanced
composition is not
lacking in unusual
or even bizarre
aspects: in the
foreground, four
Doctors of the
Church are intent
on their discussion
of the dogma of the
Immaculate
Conception; in the
centre, the Virgin
and Child with
infant John the
Baptist surrounded
by six saints with
over-elaborated
expressions and
gestures. God the
Father looks down
from on high,
circled by muscular
foreshortened
cherubs sprinkling
flower petals, an
allusion to purity
and charity.

Francesco Salviati
(Francesco de'
Rossi known as),
circa 1509–1563)
*Lamentation over
the Dead Christ,*
1539–41
Oil on canvas,
222 x 193 cm

The work was
originally created
for the Venetian
monastery of
Corpus Domini
during a brief stay
in the city by the
Florentine
Mannerist painter.
An angel in flight
with the
instruments of the
Passion is caught
in an unnatural
pose above the
tightly gathered
group around
Christ's body.
Meticulous design
and delicate
colours creating
a satin effect in
the clothing
characterise the
figures with their
solemn and clear
gestures.
The figures in the
foreground appear
to be frozen in the
icy light.

121

Room XXVIII

The west side of this large rectangular room, with the original ceiling preserved, features a balcony opening over the main entrance to Palazzo Brera, designed in the late eighteenth century by the architect Giuseppe Piermarini. Throughout almost the entire nineteenth century, this room was the central section of the Gallery of Statues, exhibiting the Academy's collection of works in plaster. In the new exhibition design of the early 20th century, the room was dedicated to 17th century Emilian painting, especially to the Bologna school of the Carracci cousins, Ludovico, Agostino and Annibale, who founded the Accademia degli Incamminati, an institute for training artists, toward the end of the 16th century. The Counter-Reformation by the Catholic Church, beginning with the Council of Trent, promoted the use of figurative images to revitalise the Catholic faith. These images were to be both eloquent and decorous. In the diocese of Bologna, guided by Cardinal Paleotti, the Carracci (Annibale in particular) proposed a new idea of painting. It was one concerned with the real and the values of history, resolved in balanced, Classical compositions that would become reference models for the entire century. Two large canvases by Ludovico and Annibale Carracci arrived in Brera in 1811, along with the masterpieces of Guido Reni and Guercino, from the richly endowed painting gallery in Palazzo Sampieri on Strada Maggiore in Bologna.

Federico Barocci (1535–1612)
Martyrdom of Saint Vitalis, 1583
Oil on canvas, 302 x 268 cm

The large altarpiece by the painter from Urbino, originally in the Church of San Vitale in Ravenna, is an early example of the transposition of the new rules of painting formulated by the Counter-Reformation into a greatly stirring scene. The crowded composition is centred on the scene of the saint, turned toward the symbols of his martyrdom, being thrown into his grave alive. The diagonal position of his body is echoed in the twisting poses of his two executioners, while the other figures stand in witness to the dramatic event.

Annibale Carracci (1560–1609)
Christ and the Samaritan Woman, 1593–94
Oil on canvas, 170 x 225 cm

With a canvas of the same dimensions as that of his cousin Ludovico, this work by Annibale was one of the same group of New Testament women in Palazzo Sampieri. The encounter between Jesus and the sinful woman, taking place next to a large well, is drawing to a close. The frame is centred on the woman while Jesus sits to the right absorbed in the conversation, which is underscored by the eloquent gestures of the two monumental and well draped interlocutors. The background is occupied by an airy classical landscape of Venetian influence.

Ludovico Carracci (1555–1619)
Christ and the Canaanite Woman,
1595–1596
Oil on canvas, 170 x 225 cm

Francesco Sampieri sold this painting to
the Pinacoteca in 1811 together with *Christ
and the Samaritan Woman* by Annibale
and *Christ and the Adulteress* by Agostino

(not on display). It was part of a group of
paintings dedicated to the female figures
in the New Testament used as overdoors
in Palazzo Sampieri in Bologna.
The two monumental protagonists are
portrayed in eloquent and measured poses.
Ludovico lingers on the description of
the secondary figures and the landscape
in the background.

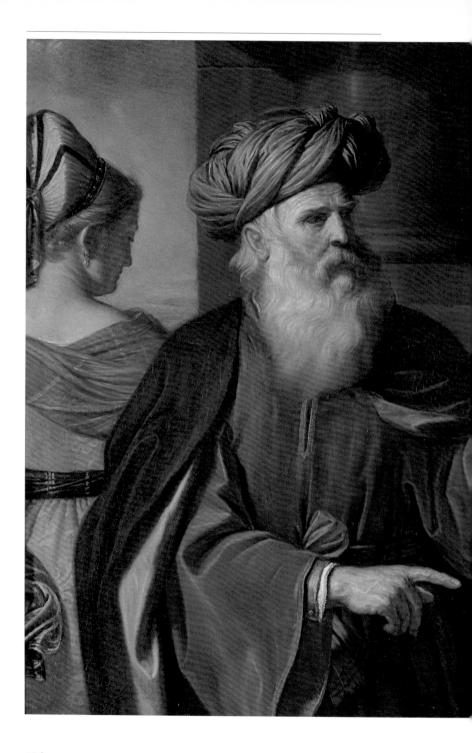

Guercino (Giovanni
Francesco Barbieri
known as),
(1591–1666)
*Abraham Casting
out Hagar and
Ishmael*
Oil on canvas,
115 x 152 cm

Another work from
the Sampieri
collection, the
painting was
commissioned in
1657 by the
municipality of
Cento for Cardinal
Lorenzo Imperiali,
legate to Ferrara.
A beautiful work
from the artist's
mature years, the
half-figure framing
indicates that the
painting was
destined for a
private collector.
Stern and
composed, the
biblical Abraham is
expelling the slave
Hagar and Ishmael,
the son they had
together, from his
house. Hagar and
Ishmael try to hold
back their grief
while Abraham's
wife, Sarah, stands
as witness to the
event with her back
to the viewer.

127

Guido Cagnacci
(1601–1663)
*The Death
of Cleopatra*
Oil on canvas,
120 x 158 cm

Cagnacci, from
Romagna, owes a
stylistic debt to
such Emilian
painters as Reni
and Guercino.
At the height of
his career, he
dedicated himself
to creating images
of women charged
with sensuality,
especially during
his sojourn with the
imperial court in
Vienna. An apt
example is this
image of Cleopatra,
who we see semi-
nude and collapsed
in an armchair after
having been bitten
by the asp.

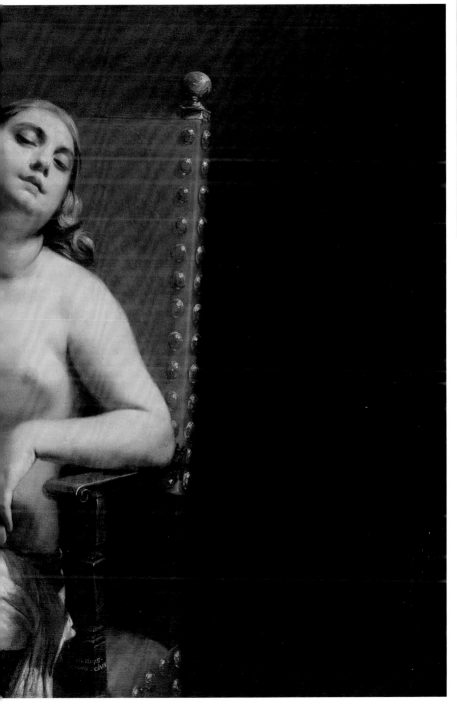

Room XXIX

Until the arrival of Giuseppe Bertini as director (1882), this room and the next were joined into a single space, later divided to increase the wall space available for hanging paintings. Including a number of highly worthy masterpieces, the works exhibited here document the important seventeenth-century current of Caravaggesque painting. The Pinacoteca has only one work by Caravaggio himself, the second and very remarkable version of *Supper at Emmaus*, painted in 1606, when the artist was already widely famous. Belonging to the Patrizi family of Rome since the seventeenth century, in 1939 it joined the Brera collection after being acquired by the Friends of Brera and thanks to the involvement of the superintendent Ettore Modigliani. Caravaggio didn't have any direct apprentice, but his well defined stylistic and compositional traits acquired a string of followers, especially in the cities where he had worked, Rome and Naples in particular. The work of the "Caravaggeschi" is characterised by an over-elaborated naturalism, light bringing out the features of the figures against a dark background, and historical settings and period clothing to re-propose the sacred episode within a historical context. The styles range from the Classical and elegant naturalism of the Tuscan Orazio Gentileschi to the personal and dramatic interpretation of the Neapolitan Battistello Caracciolo, the overstated realism of the Spaniard Jusepe de Ribera, and the tenebrous naturalism of Calabrian Mattia Preti.

Orazio Gentileschi (1563–1639)
The Holy Martyrs Cecilia, Valerian and Tiburtius Visited by an Angel
1607
Oil on canvas, 350 x 218 cm

The work comes from the church of Santa Cecilia in Como. There are a number of references to Caravaggio in the elegant composition still marked by a Mannerist approach. These include the angel and the luminism of the scene in which the young spouses are ready to receive the crown of flowers symbolising their union and the palm frond that prefigures their martyrdom. Traits proper to Gentileschi are the theatricality, the idealised figures and a cold and colour palette.

Caravaggio
(Michelangelo
Merisi known as),
(1571–1610)
Supper at Emmaus,
1605–06
Oil on canvas,
141 x 175 cm

This is one of the
major masterpieces
of the Lombard
painter, created
shortly after he was
forced to flee Rome
accused of murder.
Caravaggio
underscores the
psychological
reaction of the
characters in the
biblical episode:
in the half-darkness
of the setting,
Christ, fully mature
and bearing the
signs of his
suffering, has
just broken and
blessed the bread.
His disciples –
recognising him –
are dumbstruck.
The host and old
servant are
witnesses to the
event, unaware of
its meaning.
The shaft of light
exalts the faces,
gestures and the
few elements
composing the still-
life on the white
tablecloth.

Luca Giordano (1634–1705)
Self-Portrait as a Chemist, 1650
Oil on canvas, 116 x 96 cm

In Brera since 1855, this work from the
painter's younger years belongs to Pietro
Oggioni's bequest. Giordano portrays
himself here in the guise of an alchemist,
a subject of interest for many Neapolitan
intellectuals at the time. The cold light
sharply emphasizes the handsome face in
a three-quarter pose, plays over the details
of the clothing and illuminates the large
alembic deftly held in his hands.

Battistello Caracciolo (Giovan Battista Caracciolo known as), (1578–1635)
Christ and the Samaritan Woman, 1620–22
Oil on canvas, 200 x 165 cm

This painting, acquired by Brera in 1820 in an exchange, was attributed to Caravaggio up to the early years of the twentieth century, despite the fact that it bears the unmistakable signature of the Neapolitan Caracciolo. Battistello adopted a Caravaggesque style early on and understood the principal aspects of the Lombard painter's style better than others. Here the artist highlights the common beauty and rustic manners of the Samaritan who is about to offer water to Jesus. The strong light exalts the warm and juxtaposed colours of the woman's yellow dress and the red tunic worn by Christ.

Mattia Preti
(1613–1699)
Saint Peter and the Tribute Money
Oil on canvas,
143 x 193 cm

The biblical episode was probably painted while the Calabrian painter was in Rome. Along with *A Mother Entrusts her Children to Christ*, it belonged to the Arese Collection and was donated to Brera in 1812 by viceroy Eugène de Beauharnais. Preti simplifies a number of aspects of Caravaggesque painting: in the close-up scene, the light uniformly draws out of the shadows people wearing contemporary clothing, almost transforming the sacred scene into a profane subject.

Room XXX

Dedicated to Lombard painting from the early 17th century, the room exhibits only a limited selection of masterpieces. Due to lack of sufficient space, the rest of the abundant collection has been placed in either internal or external storage. At the beginning of the 1600s, after the first generation of artists from the period following the Council of Trent had passed on, the "Duomo factory" of Milan commissioned Cerano to do two series of large-format canvases about the life and miracles of Carlo Borromeo (the occasion was Borromeo's beatification in 1602 and his canonisation in 1610), which would be fundamental landmarks for Lombard art of those years. Giulio Cesare Procaccini joined in the effort for the second series, he too working with Morazzone and Daniele Crespi, among the luminaries of the fruitful decades in Milanese arts when Cardinal Federico Borromeo – the founder of the Biblioteca and Accademia Ambrosiana and an avid collector – was the Archbishop.

The *Martyrdom of the Saints Rufina and Seconda*, also known as *Three-Handed Painting*, is the outcome of the joint efforts of Cerano, Morazzone and Procaccini and a powerful image destined for private devotion. The highly personal Caravaggesque interpretation by Tanzio da Varallo, engaged principally on the Sacro Monte in Valsesia, is represented here with two vigorous portraits and with the *Martyrdom of the Franciscans in Nagasaki*. The great popularity of devotional images of saints in ecstasy is documented in two dramatic works with Saint Francis.

Morazzone (Pier Francesco Mazzuchelli known as), (1573–1626), Cerano (Giovan Battista Crespi known as), (1577 *circa* – 1632), Giulio Cesare Procaccini (1574–1625) *Martyrdom of the Saints Rufina and Seconda*, (*Three-Handed Painting*), 1620–25 Oil on canvas, 192 x 192 cm

In 1625, this highly important painting was in the collection of the patrician Scipione Toso, who was its likely patron. It then passed into the collection of Cardinal Cesare Monti, a part of which was acquired by Brera in 1896. Designed by Morazzone but painted by all three artists, it is an exercise in stylistic ability and also a sort of manifesto of the Milan school of painting. It was Morazzone's hand that created the dark killer in the centre, the dynamic force behind the composition. Cerano is responsible for the zone to the left with the knight and Saint Seconda already decapitated on the ground. Lastly, the portion on the right with the languid Saint Rufina and the angel comforting her is the work of Procaccini.

Cerano (Giovan Battista Crespi known as), (1577 *circa* – 1632)
Madonna of the Rosary, 1618–25
Oil on canvas, 275 x 218 cm

The altarpiece comes from the church of the suppressed Dominican convent of San Lazzaro alle Monache in Milan. The rigorous compositional layout, with the Virgin appearing before Saint Dominic, is in line with illustrious 16th-century models and a refined example of Counter-Reformationist devotional art. The lifelike characters, whose gestures and expressions are immediately clear, mark the painting's conformity to the catechesis promoted by Cardinal Federico Borromeo. The musical angels are almost literal citations of Raphael and Lotto.

Giulio Cesare Procaccini (1574–1625)
Mystical Marriage of Saint Catherine, 1620–25
Oil on canvas, 149 x 145 cm

In this painting, which also belonged to Cardinal Monti's collection, the painter, born in Bologna but resettling in Milan, resolves the softness of Correggio's style in a new, "baroque" key. The image is characterised by a fluid interplay of the heads and hands of the two orders of figures and by the somewhat Mannerist elegance of the clothing and hair.

Daniele Crespi (1597/1600–1630)
Last Supper, 1620–28
Oil on canvas, 335 x 220 cm

The large altarpiece comes from the Benedictine church of Santi Pietro e Paolo in Brugora near Besana Brianza. In composing this austere scene, Cerano's apprentice uses as his reference the *Last Supper* by Gaudenzio Ferrari in the church of Santa Maria della Passione (1544) and the decorative complexes in the chapels of the Lombard and Piedmontese Sacri Monti. Christ and the Apostles are gathered around the table laid for a feast, which is described down to the details of the crockery. The ultimate reference is to the *Last Supper* by Leonardo, the authentic prototype for this theme.

PANEM ANGELORVM MANDVCAVIT HOMO

Room XXXI

Once a single space with the two smaller adjacent rooms, up until 1882 this room was the final gallery on the path through the Pinacoteca. It now contains 17th-century paintings, sacred scenes and genre works from various contexts, Italian and Flemish, mainly in Baroque style. Works by the Flemings Rubens, Van Dyck and Jordaens entered the Brera collections in 1813 in an exchange with the Louvre for a group of paintings obtained two years earlier. With great scenographic impact, the large panel with the *Last Supper* by Pieter Rubens fills the wall where the passages to the smaller rooms are located, while on the opposite wall we find a masterpiece by Pietro da Cortona, one of the greatest exponents of the Roman Baroque. Among the still-lifes, a genre of painting that enjoyed great success in the seventeenth century, two paintings by Evaristo Baschenis stand out, perfectly representative of his oeuvre and his predilection for compositions with musical instruments and the interiors of kitchens. A relatively recent acquisition is the *Vanitas* by the German Joseph Heintz the Younger, in which the theme of love is curiously associated with fantastic creatures and objects that symbolise time and the fleeting nature of things.

Pieter Paul Rubens (1577–1640)
Last Supper, 1631–32
Oil on panel, 304 x 250 cm

Essentially by the hand of Rubens but with some marginal contributions from his bottega, the painting comes from the chapel of the Most Holy Sacrament in the cathedral of Mechelen and belongs to the late phase in the Flemish artist's career.

The dynamism of the scene is influenced by the painting style in the Veneto region in the latter part of the 16th century. In the shadows of the room, Christ blesses the bread and wine. Judas, in the foreground, nervously turns toward the viewer, while a dog under the table gazes out of the frame. The vigorous Apostles evidence their individual reactions through their expressions and postures.

Anthony van Dyck (1599–1641)
Madonna and Child with Saint Anthony of Padua, 1630–32
Oil on canvas, 189 x 158 cm

The beautiful work was executed during the painter's second sojourn in his native Antwerp after the long period spent in Italy, and particularly in Genoa, a period marked by a string of successes, especially in his portraiture. In addressing the sacred subject, Van Dyck seeks a naturalness in his figures and forthright colour tones, which recall the work of Titian and 16th-century Venetian art. The frame is the same one that held the painting when it arrived from Paris in 1813.

Pietro da Cortona (Pietro Berrettini known as), (1596–1669)
Madonna and Child with the Saints John the Baptist, Felix of Cantalice, Andrew and Catherine, 1629–30
Oil on canvas, 296 x 205 cm

The chromatically festive altarpiece arrived in the museum from the Capuchin church of Amandola, near Ascoli Piceno in The Marches.

The Tuscan architect and painter may have created it for the Capuchin Antonio Barberini, brother of Pope Urban VIII, from whom he received important commissions in Rome. The lifted curtain reveals the Madonna with Child seated on a cylindrical podium with a Classical colonnade behind them. They are surrounded by saints, whose elegant gestures contribute to underscoring the balanced theatrical orchestration of the scene.

Evaristo Baschenis (1617–1677)
Still-life with Musical Instruments
Oil on canvas, 60 x 88 cm

In this masterpiece from the 1660s, the
Bergamascan artist, specialised in still-lifes
with musical instruments, symbol of the
vanity of earthly things, evidences in filtered
light the various objects arranged almost
concentrically around a small chest.
The asymmetrical composition is balanced
by the velvet curtain. The blemished fruit
and veil of dust on the mandola allude
symbolically to the passage of time and
to death.

Bernardo Strozzi (1581–1644)
*Portrait of a Knight of Malta (Scipione
Papafava)*, 1620–25
Oil on canvas, 129 x 98 cm

The virtuosic portrait, in the Brera
collections since 1903, is part of a generous
donation by Casimiro Sipriot. The person
portrayed has been identified as Scipione
Papafava, Knight of Malta, who conducted
a brilliant career in the military.
The composition of this portrait, created by
the Genoese painter after moving to Venice,
is reminiscent of those done by Van Dyck
in Genoa. The clothing and sceptre,
painted with mellow colours, underscore
the social status of the subject, while
the realistically rendered face and relaxed
pose evoke his personality.

Rooms XXXII-XXXIII

These two small rooms were designed in 1950 by Piero Portaluppi to house paintings from the Flemish and Dutch schools of the 16th and first half of the 17th centuries. The works are prevalently small-format portraits and landscapes, which were acquired gradually over the years through purchases and exchanges, but particularly with the Oggioni bequest in 1855. The intimate dimensions, lowered ceiling and parquet floor aim to evoke the cosy rooms in northern European patrician estates. Among the early 16th-century Flemish works is the exceptional triptych by Jan de Beer – acquired by the museum in 1808 along with other paintings seized from the Venetian churches – the tempera attributed to the same artist with the rare northern European iconography of *Saint Luke Painting the Virgin*, and *Saint Catherine* by the Master of Female Half Figures. Among the portraits, outstanding for its quality is the *Dame*, belonging to the Du Croy family of Brussels, depicted in sober widow's garb by Anthony van Dyck. The work was obtained via an exchange with the Louvre in 1813. The *Village*, a small oil-on-copper work from 1607 by Jan Brueghel the Elder, a famous Flemish painter who also worked for Cardinal Federico Borromeo, documents his bountiful production of genre scenes, in this case a village, inhabited by figurines.

Jan de Beer (1475–1520/35) *Nativity, Adoration of the Magi, Rest during the Flight into Egypt* (Triptych of the Adoration of the Magi), (detail) 1515–20

Jan de Beer
(1475–1520/35)
*Nativity, Adoration
of the Magi, Rest
during the Flight
into Egypt* (*Triptych
of the Adoration of
the Magi*), 1515–20
Oil on panel. Central
panel, 156 x 123 cm;
Side panels,
157 x 57 cm and
159 x 58 cm

The Antwerpian
painter, with the
assistance of
helpers, filled the
central panel of the
triptych with
minutely described
people and objects,
reflecting the
influence of
contemporary
Italian art in the
architectonic
backgrounds and in
a number of details.
Of particular
interest are the
moveable side
panels with a night-
time *Nativity* scene
and the everyday
atmosphere of the
Flight into Egypt, in
which much space
is dedicated to the
landscape.

Room XXXIV

With a layout dating back to the nineteenth century, the room is dedicated to 18th-century sacred painting, exhibiting mainly large-format works. Four altarpieces were obtained by Brera in 1799, during the early years of the creation of Pinacoteca, from the Milanese church of Santi Cosma e Damiano alla Scala, which was torn down to make room for the Teatro dei Filodrammatici, next to the Teatro alla Scala. They are the classically inspired works by Pompeo Batoni, Giuseppe Bottani and the Frenchman Pierre Subleyras, created in the first half of the eighteenth century in late-Baroque Rome. A number of different works document the painting of eighteenth-century Naples, including the youthful *Ecce Homo* by Luca Giordano, and that of contemporary Bologna. Among them are a rare painting of a sacred subject (*Crucifixion*) by Giuseppe Maria Crespi and *Saint Francis Receiving the Stigmata* by Ubaldo Gandolfi, marked by a luminous colour scheme à la Tiepolo. The upper part of an entire wall is occupied by the huge large-format canvas (*telero*) by the young Giambattista Tiepolo, *The Madonna of Mount Carmel*. Broken into two parts after being removed from the church, the two portions were acquired in Paris in 1925 by the Chiesa family and promptly donated to the Pinacoteca, where they were rejoined.

Sebastiano Ricci (1659–1734) *Martyrdom of Saint Erasmus*, 1694–97 Oil on canvas, 118 x 95 cm

Acquired in 1978 from an antique dealer in Genoa, the canvas has been attributed to the Venetian painter Sebastiano Ricci. The scene is rather gruesome: the bound and martyred body of the saint, protector of sailors, is accentuated in a brutal light that rips through the shadowy setting and lingers on the tunics and muscular arms of the executioners, who are turning a windlass (the saint's attribute) to tear out the saint's viscera.

Giambattista Tiepolo (1696–1770)
The Madonna of Mount Carmel, 1721–27
Oil on canvas, 210 x 650 cm

The work celebrating Carmelite devotion was located in the Venetian church of Sant'Aponal. The Madonna is giving the large scapular to Saint Simon Stock, while baby Jesus gives a smaller one to Saint Teresa of Avila. On the left, the souls in Purgatory are comforted by a flying angel. On the right, the prophet Elijah, who chose Mount Carmel in Palestine as his earthly abode. The saturated colours reflect the young Venetian painter's skill in the Tenebrism technique in vogue in the early eighteenth century.

Pompeo Batoni
(1708–1787)
*Madonna and Child
with the Saints
Joseph, Zachariah,
Elisabeth and
young John the
Baptist*, 1737–40
Oil on canvas,
403 x 288 cm

The large
altarpiece,
originally in the
Church of Santi
Cosma e Damiano
alla Scala, well
illustrates Pompeo
Batoni's academic
style. He was a
successful artist
in eighteenth-
century Rome,
where he painted
extraordinary
portraits of foreign
travellers on their
Grand Tours.
The characters
here, exhibiting
the influence of
Raphael and the
seventeenth-
century Emilian
painters, are drawn
with crisp features
and organised in
a balanced scheme
in front of columns
in perspective
and an imaginary
landscape.

156

Pierre Subleyras
(1699–1749)
*Crucifixion with
Magdalene, Saint
Eusebius and Saint
Philip Neri*, 1744
Oil on canvas,
408 x 232 cm

Signed and dated
at bottom centre by
the French painter,
the work is part
of an important
nucleus of paintings
from the destroyed
Milanese church
of Santi Cosma e
Damiano. Painted
in Rome, where the
artist had long
resided, the work
shows a Classical
composition.
Three worshippers
have come to show
devotion to Christ
on the Cross.
Their earnest
poses create a
symmetrical
balance: Eusebius
stands with his
arms outstretched
while Magdalene
and Philip kneel
with clasped hands.

Rooms XXXV-XXXVI

In 1950, when the Pinacoteca reopened after the Second World War, two new oblong rooms were created by partitioning a rectangular room. The work was carried out on designs by the architect Piero Portaluppi and under the direction of Fernanda Wittgens. The new spaces give onto a corridor through two elliptical archways supported on columns from the storerooms of the Opificio delle Pietre Dure in Florence, evoking eighteenth-century Rococo interiors. The rooms are used to display the "quadri da stanza" (paintings made to be hung in private houses) produced in Venice and other Italian centres of art in the 18th century, destined mainly for private collectors. The museum obtained most of them in the 20th century.

In Room XXXV, a series of extraordinary masterpieces bear witness to the development of genre paintings and vedute of Venice. The matching views of Venice offered by Canaletto and Francesco Guardi are flanked by two beautiful, rare Lombard vedute by Bernardo Bellotto. The two elegant scenes of daily life by Pietro Longhi are paired with the portrait of Marianna Carlevarijs done in pastel.

Room XXXVI, on the other hand, features portraits, with a number of important works by the Bergamascan Fra' Galgario and the Genoese Alessandro Magnasco, but especially with the Brescian Pitocchetto's intense *Porters* (errand boys), which enjoyed significant success in a society quite concerned with the social themes promoted by the illuminist culture. These paintings are flanked by two of the painter's still-lifes. Other significant examples of genre painting are the *Fair* by Giuseppe Maria Crespi of Bologna, the *Old Woman and the Boy* by the Neapolitan Gaspare Traversi and the figure studies by the Milanese Francesco Londonio.

Pietro Longhi (1702–1785)
The Tooth-Puller
Oil on canvas, 50 x 62 cm

Dated to the period 1746–52, the painting became part of the Brera collections in 1911. With disenchanted irony, the Venetian painter, specialised in small-format genre paintings, portrays an episode in front of the Doge's Palace from day-to-day Venetian life. The would-be dentist proudly brandishes the tooth extracted from his agonising young patient, who is seated before him. Passersby of various social levels watch and react to the scene: ladies in couples, knights in half-masks, common women and children. The seated woman intones good luck charms while the dwarf makes the sign of the horns to ward off misfortune.

Giovanni Battista
Piazzetta
(1683–1754)
*Rebecca and
Eleazar at the Well*
Oil on canvas,
102 x 137 cm

Donated by Emilio
Treves in 1921, the
painting is known to
have been in the
Alvise Contarini
Collection at the
Madonna dell'Orto
in Venice, paired
with a *Judith and
Holofernes*, which
is now in a private
collection. Dated to
1735–40, the work
portrays the biblical
episode of the
meeting at the well
between Abraham's
messenger, Eleazar,
and the future wife
of Isaac, Rebecca.
The characters
dressed in
fashionable
eighteenth-century
clothes, the half-
figure composition
and the light and
luminous colour
palette almost
transfigure the
sacred subject into
a pastoral scene.

Canaletto (Giovanni Antonio Canal known as), (1697–1768)
View of the Grand Canal from Campo Sant'Ivo toward Punta della Dogana, 1740–45
Oil on canvas, 53 x 70 cm

Acquired at a Christie's auction in London in 1928, it was painted, like its companion *View of the San Marco Basin from the* *Punta della Dogana*, before the painter left for England. This veduta is one of the highly acclaimed versions of the same subject, which was extremely popular among Canaletto's contemporaries.
The palazzi facing onto the canal, populated with gondolas and sailboats, are rendered with great optical precision in a limpid, timeless light.

Francesco Guardi (1712–1793)
*The Grand Canal with the Fabbriche Nuove
at the Rialto*
Oil on canvas, 56 x 75 cm

Together with its companion, *The Grand
Canal toward Rialto with Palazzo Grimani
and Palazzo Manin,* this painting is part of
the Oggioni bequest, whose last painting

arrived at Brera in 1855. Dated to just after
the mid 1750s, it belongs to an early phase
in the painter's career, when he was still
strongly influenced by Canaletto, especially
in the work's broad perspective. But
Guardi's own distinctive style is seen in the
fringed brushstrokes, bolder shadows and
darkened waters with gondolas and other
boats guided by darting faceless figures.

Bernardo Bellotto
(1721–1780)
View of Gazzada
Oil on canvas,
64.5 x 98.5 cm

Together with the
*View of Villa
Perabò-Melzi*, this
is one of the
greatest
achievements of
eighteenth-century
European veduta
painting. It is the
work of Canaletto's
nephew and
apprentice during
his sojourn in
Lombardy in the
early 1740s, before
he moved to
Dresden in 1744.
The painter
animates the crisply
rendered woodland
village with
washerwomen and
farmers hard at
work at a particular
time of day,
underscored by
the vibrant light.
Bellotto's modern
vedute are
distinguished by
their sincere
observance of
the reality of the
modern landscape
and precise
indications of time.

Fra Galgario (Vittore Ghislandi known as),
(1655–1743)
Portrait of Count Flaminio Tassi
Oil on canvas, 127 x 98 cm

Dating to circa 1715, this beautiful portrait
of a young Bergamascan nobleman shows
the subject naturally and elegantly posed
in a black, richly embroidered tailcoat.
The light-coloured wig on his shaven
head accentuates the genuine and vivid
expressivity of the young man's
countenance. In this and many other
portraits, Ghislandi achieves an acute
analysis of his subject, bringing out the
personality and psychology of each person
through his or her physiognomy and posture.

Giacomo Ceruti (1698–1767)
Porter Sitting with a Basket, Eggs and Poultry
Oil on canvas, 130 x 95 cm

Together with its companion, *Porter Sitting
on a Basket*, this painting, dating to *circa*
1735, is among Ceruti's masterpieces.
This was a painter who paid significant
attention to the more humble strata of
society. Painted for the collection of the
Oratorian father, Giulio Barbisoni of Brescia,
the work was donated to the Pinacoteca in
1968 by Giovanni Testori. The light clearly
defines the young farm boy resting on a
stone and gazing at the viewer with a pained
expression, too tired to continue carrying
the large basket over his shoulder.

Rooms XXXVII-XXXVIII

The painting of the 19th century, which witnessed the birth of the Brera Academy of Fine Arts and the Pinacoteca, while representing a significant part of the collections, is necessarily restricted in the last two rooms. A number of important paintings from the century were obtained as bequests from the Academy, joining with the contest submissions that were acquired steadily over time, and when the two institutions were divided, they remained on display in the Pinacoteca. Hundreds of works were deposited in other facilities due to lack of space. The exhibition design of 2009 exalts on two walls a highly select group of masterpieces of Neoclassical and Romantic painting, restores the proper perceptual space to the grandiose *Fiumana* by Giuseppe Pellizza da Volpedo, and mixes fundamental works of Italian Realism from the latter half of the nineteenth century with lesser known paintings that nevertheless document an important figurative history, such as *Sad Presentiment* by Girolamo Induno and the landscapes of Ciardi and Gignous. Lombard Neoclassicism is represented in paintings by Andrea Appiani and Giuseppe Bossi, among the first to work for the creation of the Pinacoteca. The former is represented by four ovals created as overdoors for the Milanese dwelling of Francesco Melzi d'Eril, the latter by the curious *Self-Portrait with Gaetano Cattaneo, Giuseppe Taverna and Carlo Porta*. Also worthy of mention is the *Portrait of Giovanni Battista Sommariva* by Pierre Prud'hon. Francesco Hayez, protagonist of Italian Romanticism and professor of painting at the Brera Academy, is represented with a number of masterpieces, which document his success in embracing a number of different genres. Lastly, on the free wall of Room XXXVIII the visit concludes with the amazing *Spring Pastures* by the divisionist Segantini.

Giuseppe Bossi (1777–1815)
Burial of Themistocle's Ashes
Oil on panel, 60 x 119 cm

Painted for the first exhibition held at the Brera Academy, Bossi's small-format panel portrays the rare historical subject of the exequies of the Athenian commander, who committed suicide during his unjust exile. People dressed in ancient garb are gathered in distinct groups around the grave in a composition similar to classical bas-reliefs or those sculpted by Bossi's friend Antonio Canova.

Francesco Hayez (1791–1882)
The Kiss, 1859
Oil on canvas, 112 x 88 cm

This is one of the icons of the Pinacoteca, perhaps one of the best loved works in all of 19th-century Italian painting. It became immediately popular after being presented at the Brera exhibition of 1859. The romantic image of a young couple in Medieval clothing united in a passionate kiss is also an allegory for the close alliance between Italy and France during the Italian Wars of Independence. The colours of the clothing, rendered with material realism, recall those of the flags of the two nations.

Francesco Hayez (1791–1882)
Portrait of Alessandro Manzoni, 1841
Oil on canvas, 120 x 92.5 cm

Together with the *Portrait of Teresa Manzoni Borri Stampa*, this work was donated to Brera in the early 20th century by Stefano Stampa, stepson of the great writer. In order to achieve as natural a portrayal as possible, the painter subjected the reserved Manzoni to a full fifteen sittings. The end result is a sober portrait with prevalently dark tones in line with the writer's personality. Manzoni is seated on a chair against the neutral background of a wall, absorbed in his thoughts.

Silvestro Lega
(1826–1895)
The Pergola (*Early
Afternoon*), 1868
Oil on canvas,
75 x 93.5 cm

The painting was
donated to the
museum by the
Friends of Brera
Association in 1931.
In this work, the
painter, one of the
Macchiaioli, exalts
the modern lifestyle
of the Tuscan
middle class in the
latter half of the
nineteenth century.
Under the leafy
pergola, which
provides shade
pierced by fine
beams of sunlight, a
group of women are
about to have their
post-prandial
coffee on a sultry
summer day.

Giovanni Fattori (1825–1908)
The Red Wagon, 1887
Oil on canvas, 88 x 170 cm

This major painting from the Turinese collection of Riccardo Gualino was acquired in 1937 by initiative of Ettore Modigliani. Another of the Tuscan Macchiaioli painters, Fattori resolves the theme of the landscape and the people of the Maremma region with dense and rapid touches, to create broadly sketched colour fields: the figure of the farmer to the left, darkened in the shadow of the cart; the portion of red cart to the right; the pale masses of the two oxen in the centre; and the background of the sea and countryside set off by a clean line demarcating the border between light and shadow.

Giovanni Segantini
(1858–1899)
Spring Pastures,
1896
Oil on canvas,
95 x 155 cm

Among Segantini's
favourites, this
painting was
donated in 1957
by the Friends of
Brera. Created via
the divisionist
technique of using
patches of pure
colour, the painting
is characterised by
a great luminosity.
The alpine pasture
coming back to life
in the springtime,
with the cow and
her calf grazing in
the foreground,
hides other
symbolic meanings.
The bond between
the two animals
exalts the theme
of motherhood,
proposed here in
the idyllic setting of
the simple country
life.

Giuseppe Pelizza da Volpedo (1868–1907)
Fiumana, 1895–96
Oil on canvas, 255 x 438 cm

The enormous unfinished canvas, donated by the Sprind company in 1986, was a fundamental step in the development of the famous *The Fourth Estate*, now part of the collections of the Galleria d'Arte Moderna in Milan and a true artistic, political and social manifesto of the late nineteenth-century Italian proletariat. The divisionist painter addresses the theme of labour by painting this endless flow of striking farm-workers moving through the piazza of Volpedo, led by life-sized figures representing – in tune with the bountiful season of Symbolism – youth, manhood, old age and motherhood.

Bibliography

The History of Palazzo di Brera

A. Scotti, *Brera 1776-1815. Nascita e sviluppo di una istituzione culturale milanese*, Florence 1979.

S. Bonamico, A. Scotti, *Progetto Brera*, Pordenone 1985, pp. 13-79.

The Pinacoteca Collections

R. Tardito, *Brera: Storia della Pinacoteca e delle sue collezioni*, Florence 1986.

P.C. Marani, *Leonardo e i leonardeschi a Brera*, Florence 1988.

S. Coppa, *La pittura lombarda del Sei e del Settecento nella Pinacoteca di Brera*, Florence 1988.

Pinacoteca di Brera. Scuole lombarda e piemontese 1300-1535, Milan 1988.

P. Humfrey, *La pittura veneta del Quattrocento nella Pinacoteca di Brera*, Florence 1989.

Pinacoteca di Brera. Scuole lombarda, ligure e piemontese 1535-1769, Milan 1989.

Pinacoteca di Brera. Scuola veneta, Milan 1990.

Pinacoteca di Brera. Scuola emiliana, Milan 1991.

Pinacoteca di Brera. Scuole dell'Italia centrale e meridionale, Milan 1992.

Pinacoteca di Brera. Dipinti dell'Ottocento e del Novecento. Collezioni dell'Accademia e della Pinacoteca, Milan 1993-1994.

Pinacoteca di Brera. Scuole straniere, Milan 1995.

Pinacoteca di Brera. Addenda e apparati generali, Milan 1996.

Brera. Un milanese che parlava toscano. Lamberto Vitali e la sua collezione, exhibition catalogue, Milan 2001.

Per Brera. Collezionisti e doni alla Pinacoteca dal 1882 al 2000, edited by M. Ceriana, C. Quattrini, Florence 2004.

S. Bandera (ed.), *Brera la Pinacoteca: storia e capolavori*, Milan 2009.

S. Sicoli (ed.), *Milano 1809. La Pinacoteca di Brera e i musei in età napoleonica*, Milan 2010.

The Directors of the Pinacoteca

Dizionario biografico dei Soprintendenti Storici dell'arte (1904-1974), Bologna 2007.

Further informations

Entrance
Via Brera 28, from the Court of Honour,
1st floor
Access for wheelchairs, Via Fiori Oscuri 2

Opening Hours
Tuesday-Sunday 8:30-19:15
The ticket office closes at 18:40
Closed Mondays and on January 1st,
May 1st and December 25th

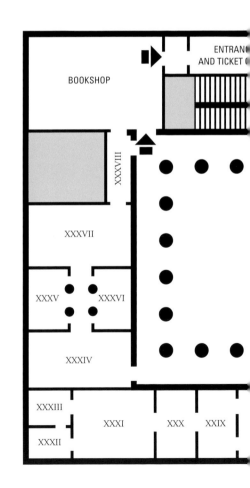

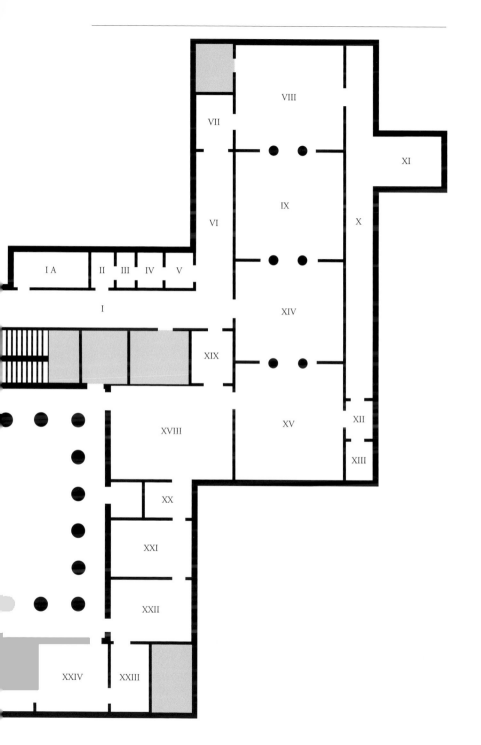